# F-8 CRUSADER
## VS
# MiG-17
## Vietnam 1965–72

PETER MERSKY

OSPREY PUBLISHING
Bloomsbury Publishing Plc

PO Box 883, Oxford, OX1 9PL, UK
1385 Broadway, 5th Floor, New York, NY 10018, USA
Email: info@ospreypublishing.com

OSPREY is a trademark of Osprey Publishing, a division of
Bloomsbury Publishing Plc

First published in Great Britain in 2014 by Osprey Publishing

Transferred to digital print-on-demand in 2019

Printed and bound in Great Britain

A CIP catalogue record for this book is available from the British Library

ISBN: 978 1 78200 810 1
PDF ISBN: 978 1 78200 811 8
ePub ISBN: 978 1 78200 812 5

Edited by Tony Holmes
Cover artworks and battlescene by Gareth Hector
Three-views, cockpits, armament scrap views and Engaging the Enemy artwork
by Jim Laurier
Index by Sandra Shotter
Typeset in Adobe Garamond
Maps by Boundford.com
Originated by PDQ Digital Media Solutions

**The Woodland Trust**

Osprey Publishing supports the Woodland Trust, the UK's leading woodland
conservation charity.

**www.ospreypublishing.com**

To find out more about our authors and books visit our website. Here you will
find extracts, author interviews, details of forthcoming events and the option to
sign-up for our newsletter.

**Acknowledgements**

A book project like this naturally involves a lot of people, with their good will
and desire helping make the final product the best it can be. First and foremost
is Col D. J. Kiely, USMC (Ret.), a long-time friend and a highly experienced
F-8 and RF-8 pilot. Barrett Tillman and Dr. Frank Olynyk, two acknowledged
aviation historians, were also important supporters, as were Dale J. Gordon and
Archie DiFante at the US Navy History and Heritage Command's Naval
Aviation Historian's Office, and the US Air Force Historical Research Activity,
respectively, and Rand Bethea of USAF Air Combat Command. Rear Adm
Tom Irwin, USNR (Ret.), a former CO and long-time friend, answered my
technical questions on the F-8. Thank you also to Tom Corboy, Al Lansdowne
and Robert Walters for their help with the Engaging the Enemy text. Thanks to
Capt Richard Schaffert, USN (Ret.) and Lt Cdr John Laughter, USNR (Ret.),
"Brown Bear Lead" and "Brown Bear 2", respectively, Col Ron Lord, USAF
(Ret.), Col Will Abbott, USAF (Ret.), Randy Rime and Cdr Cole Pierce, USN
(Ret.) for their specific, and patient help with formation diagram caption.

The largest block of friends and helpers is the many former Crusader aviators
and squadron members and their families, all wishing to preserve the aviator's
story. This group includes the many readers and former F-8 pilots, themselves,
who make up the very active Crusader website, always ready to put in their
stories, opinions and good-natured ribbing. And Dick Atkins and Roger Stites of
the LTV Retirees Club who helped with specific photographic research. Tom
Chee also contributed important information on specific F-8s. As always, Cdr
Doug Siegfried, US Navy (Ret.) of the Tailhook Association was ready to provide
photographic assistance. Dr. István Toperczer, a long-time friend and fellow
Vietnam historian, is a very fine photographer, author and researcher who has
become the expert on that country's story in the air. Besides contributing quite a
few photographs from his collection, he also helped with the more personal side
of the story, giving insights into individual pilots, whose identities were rarely
known in such detail during the war and have only just now, mainly through his
efforts, been more publicized. Fellow Osprey author Peter Davies shared a lot of
information about the MiG-17 and the Vietnamese Peoples' Air Force (VPAF)
in general. And a special thanks to long-time friend and fellow author/editor
Harold Livingston. And in the background is always Tony Holmes, another
long-time friend and editor. A highly experienced author and well-traveled
aviation writer himself, Tony remains the foundation of Osprey's successful line
of aviation books. Having produced many on his own, he truly understands
production from both sides of the aisle, author and publisher. He is largely
responsible for the look and success of many of the company's aviation books.

**F-8 Crusader cover art**

On July 21, 1967, Lt Cdr Tim Hubbard of VF-211, embarked in USS *Bon
Homme Richard* (CVA-34), was part of a strike against petroleum storage facilities
at Ta Xa, northwest of Haiphong. His original F-8C "went down", however, and
he had to jump into another Crusader armed for flak suppression duties with one
AIM-9 on the upper port rail and six Zuni canisters on the remaining rails, two
on each rail. Undeterred, he launched as the escort for Lt Cdr T. R. Swartz and
his wingman, flying A-4C Skyhawks in the anti-SAM role. They briefed that
Hubbard would watch Swartz' "six" but would detach if MiGs appeared. A call of
"Bandits! Bandits!" came from someone in the main pack, followed by a call
directly to Swartz – "'Pouncers', you have a couple of MiGs behind you!"
('Pouncer' was the A-4 *Iron Hand* section's call sign). Swartz quickly looked
behind him and, sure enough, *eight* MiG-17s were closing fast. "Get 'em,
Gators!" he called as he watched Hubbard break away as briefed. F-8s and MiGs
mixed it up as Sidewinders and cannon fire filled the sky. Hubbard fired his only
Sidewinder, which failed to guide and missed, leaving him with the six Zunis and
his cannon. He pursued the MiG, firing the Zunis on the starboard side and,
finally, as shown here, on the lower port side. These last two rockets did some
damage, but the MiG kept flying. As Hubbard fired his cannon, his adversary
ejected from his mortally wounded fighter just before it blew up. This kill was
the seventh, and last, for VF-211. (Cover artwork by Gareth Hector)

**MiG-17 cover art**

The first engagement between Crusaders and MiGs occurred on April 3, 1965,
when MiG-17s of the VPAF's 921st Fighter Regiment attacked a US Navy strike
force hitting bridges at Ham Rung. Eight fighters, led by Capt Pham Ngoc Lan
in MiG "Red 2310", took off from Noi Bai, northwest of Hanoi. It was not long
before the communist pilots spotted the Americans and attacked. Ngoc Lan
lined up on the VF-211 jet flown by Lt Cdr Spence Thomas and fired his three
heavy cannon, striking the gray F-8 around the cockpit and wings. Thomas
struggled to keep his Crusader flying, his North Vietnamese opponent convinced
that he had mortally damaged the US Navy fighter. However, Ngoc Lan had to
break off the engagement and return to base because his MiG was low on fuel.
Indeed, he eventually had to crash land on the banks of the Duong River – the
MiG was later returned to service. Ngoc Lan's gun camera film seemed to show
that the F-8 had been destroyed, and accordingly he received credit for the
VPAF's first kill. However, as it turned out, Lt Cdr Thomas was able to nurse his
badly damaged fighter to the large base at Da Nang, in South Vietnam.
Incredibly, the Crusader was repaired and went on to enjoy a lengthy career
before being taken out of service after the war. (Cover artwork by Gareth Hector)

# CONTENTS

# INTRODUCTION

Vietnam surprised America. We were not ready for it either psychologically or strategically. The similarities between that war and how America was set up to enter World War II are very close. In 1941, although we had been watching with great interest the growing conflict in Europe between Nazi Germany and the rest of the Continent, we did not want to become involved short of sending arms and materiel to the beleaguered countries that were losing the fight, sometimes in very quick time. By December 1941, only feisty little Britain stood against the mighty German juggernaut.

The same was true in Asia. Who would have believed that the island nation of Japan could swallow the giant country of China and the distant island nations in the Pacific, although China was beset by war-lord-driven civil war and growing communist infestation? We chose to offer occasional loads of obsolete aircraft and bags of food to the victims of incredibly brutal Japanese aggression in Nanking and Shanghai and look the other way.

Some 20 years later, we knew the communists were on the march, steamrolling their way down the Southeast Asian peninsula with little opposition except, perhaps, for the poorly organized French who suffered a great defeat at Dien Bien Phu in 1954, thereby nearly eliminating Franco influence in the region except for aristocratic retention of the language and occasional French city names. Aside from occasional American patrols along the South China Sea coastlines and, again, the donation of obsolescent aircraft like PB4Y Privateers and F8F Bearcats, countries like South Vietnam and Thailand were on their own.

Not only were there similarities in the wars themselves, but also in the philosophies of equipment, especially in respect to the aircraft involved. A poor, Third World country like North Vietnam did not have the money or internal resources with which to develop a first-rate air force, or the aircraft to equip it. Like so many communist "colonies", North Vietnam quickly fell under the sway of the Soviet Union and communist China. The Soviets sent in MiG fighters or brought North Vietnamese student pilots to Russia to undergo training in the MiG-17s that were entering service at bases near Hanoi and Haiphong. The growth rate of the Vietnamese Peoples' Air Force (VPAF) was very high, although many of the neophyte MiG pilots had never seen heavier machinery beyond a farm tractor. The concepts of aerial tactics and aerial discipline were also foreign to them, and they had to be learned along with the actual mechanics of flying. These qualities had already been made part of the long and intense training experienced by US Naval Aviators by the time they arrived on station off North and South Vietnam.

The MiG-17 was barely a third generation design, although its ancestor MiG-15 had given a very good account of itself in the Korean War of 1950-53. Going up against US Air Force (USAF) F-86 Sabres and US Navy/Marine Corps F9F Panthers, and often flown not only by North Korean and Chinese pilots but by Russian surrogates "volunteered" to meet American aviators in the first jet aerial combats, the high-tailed MiGs were not to be taken lightly.

An F-8E of VF-162 armed with four AIM-9Bs is prepared for launch from *Oriskany* in 1965. (Rick Adams)

However, by the mid-1960s, the American attitude toward the aging MiG-17s and the superiority of fourth-generation US jet fighters led American pilots to adopt a false air of confidence that sometimes caught up with them. Certainly, Vought's world-beater F-8 Crusader, sleek and fast and carrying an armament of four 20mm cannon and up to four advanced AIM-9 Sidewinder aerial missiles, could make short work of the aging MiGs reported to be part of the VPAF.

But, unfortunately, such was not the case and the highly maneuverable, tough little Soviet fighters often took on the F-8, and its stablemate F-4 Phantom II, and the result was occasionally dictated by individual pilot-specific training and courage. The highly trained US Navy pilots certainly had the technical edge in their considerably newer aircraft, but sometimes the difference came down to the age-old dictate that the opposition in the MiGs were over their homeland and they were fighting a foreign invader, as they had for hundreds of years.

Readers will note I rarely discuss US Marine Corps F-8 squadrons in this volume. I wish there were stories of Crusader VMFs engaging MiG-17s but it did not happen. US Marine Corps F-8s were certainly in Southeast Asia. One squadron, VMF(AW)-212, even made one of the earliest carrier deployments in 1965 aboard USS *Oriskany* (CVA-34). However, while three other squadrons did put in a lot of time ashore at Da Nang and Chu Lai between 1965 and 1968, they were always dedicated to close air support (CAS) – definitely vital work, and often the measure between life and death for Marine and Army troops in close contact. So, try as I might, I just could not find anything about a MiG-17 engagement involving a US Marine Corps Crusader. If anyone knows something different then please contact me via the publisher.

Finally, as a lieutenant "jaygee", Jim Brady flew Crusaders with VF-62 during the 1962 Cuban Missile Crisis. He and Lt Howie Bullman were scrambled from NAS Boca Chica at Key West, Florida, to intercept two Cuban MiG-17s heading for US patrol aircraft taking photos of Soviet ships bringing ICBMs into Cuba. Flying new F-8Es, the two

Naval Aviators used their jets' APQ-94 radar to track the incoming threat. Gaining the advantage behind the MiGs, Bullman and Brady prepared to fire their Sidewinders when their controller told them to wait while "permission was asked from Washington". But permission was denied and the two disappointed Crusader pilots were directed to break off and return. Although the rules of engagement had been met when the MiGs apparently started making gun runs on the US P-2 Neptune and P-3 Orion patrol aircraft, the managers far away in the Pentagon thought it better not to risk a wider conflict.

Brady subsequently left the US Navy as a lieutenant and flew airliners for Pan Am. Although he did not fly the plane in Vietnam, the following little memoir is an important, heartfelt window into what an F-8 driver thought about his time with one of the greatest naval fighters in history:

> I have thought often why we all loved the Crusader so much. It became an extension of our minds, and the stream of consciousness that it took to fly the bird went from our brains to the aircraft. Our bodies and the movement of our limbs became part of the system. No other aircraft that I have ever flown created such an intimate relationship with its pilots.
>
> I think it is a rare relationship indeed. The plane became an extension of our thoughts and when it was right, it was as if we were the aircraft, and vice versa! It was a very challenging aircraft, and if you did not clearly understand its strengths and weaknesses, it would kill you in a second. I saw too many do just that!
>
> The Crusader was a nearly Mach 2 aircraft only ten years after we first broke the sound barrier. There were no computers or fly-by-wire systems to keep you within the VN diagram [which shows the sustained Gs vs airspeed before entering a stall]. It was up to you to keep it, not only within its engineering limits, but to take it to the very edge of those limits to best the enemy. I had some awesome dogfights with Ron Knott, my very dear friend. He and I would meet, head on, at 35,000ft and before we had to RTB [return to base] for low fuel we would be at tree-top level in a slow scissors trying to find a way to get behind the other. We would return to Cecil [Field] soaked with sweat from pulling Gs. Damn, it was great fun!

Ordnance personnel load AIM-9B Sidewinders on a VF-51 F-8E aboard *Ticonderoga* in February 1964, six months before the Gulf of Tonkin Incident. (US Navy)

# CHRONOLOGY

**1950**

**January 13** SI-2 (MiG-17 prototype) flies for the first time. Production of the fighter begins the following year at five Soviet factories to equip Warsaw Pact air forces. A total of 10,824 are built, including 1,061 in China as the Shenyang J-5.

**1952**

**September** US Navy issues a requirement for a carrier fighter capable of Mach 1.2 at 30,000ft (9144m) and Mach 0.9 at sea level. Also, a rate of climb of 25,000ft (7620m) per minute, but only a 100-kt (184km/h) landing speed. Armament to include cannon or machine guns as well as missiles, coupled with high maneuverability. Bureau of Aeronautics (BuAer) requirement goes to eight companies, of which only Douglas, Grumman and Vought had any real experience with carrier aircraft.

**1953**

**May** Vought's Model V-383 proposal was accepted.

**1955**

**March 25** XF8U-1 makes its first flight with Vought Chief Test Pilot John W. Konrad at the controls.

**1956**

**March** 110 VPAF pilots begin training in China and the USSR.

**1957**

**March** VF-32 is the first US Navy fleet squadron to receive the F8U-1.

**1960**

**Spring** 52 VPAF pilots begin MiG-17 conversion training in China.

**1962**

**December** First groups of Soviet and Chinese-trained VPAF MiG-17 pilots return to North Vietnam.

**1964**

**February 3** 36 MiG-17 and MiG-15UTI aircraft are donated to the VPAF by the USSR and used to establish the 921st Fighter Regiment (FR) "Sao Dao" (Red Star).

**August 2** In the Gulf of Tonkin Incident, North Vietnamese P-4 patrol boats attack the destroyer USS *Maddox* (DD-731) as it gathers intelligence off North Vietnam.

**August 5** US carriers begin retaliatory air strikes near Vinh. F-8 squadrons VF-51 and VF-53 from the USS *Ticonderoga* (CVA-14) provide escort cover as well as their own strike capability using Zuni 5-in. rockets.

**1965**

**March 15** US Navy flies first Operation *Rolling Thunder* missions.

**April 3** First confrontation between US Navy F-8 Crusaders and VPAF MiG-17s. VF-211 engages the 921st FR, resulting in confusing claims by the VPAF who state that at least one F-8 was shot down and another either destroyed or at least damaged as the first US kill for the VPAF. However, the pilot of the "downed" F-8 is able to recover ashore and his plane is eventually repaired and returned to flight status.

## 1966

**June 12**  F-8 scores its first kill when VF-211 CO Cdr Hal Marr shoots down one MiG-17 confirmed, and also scores a "probable," which is later confirmed by intelligence sources and even the North Vietnamese, themselves, but not by the US Navy.

**June 21**  VF-211's Lt Gene Chancy gets a MiG-17 probably with guns and squadronmate Lt(jg) Phil Vampatella downs the F-8's third MiG-17 kill, which earns him the first Navy Cross for a fighter pilot in Vietnam. In return Lt Cdr Cole Black is shot down, as well as Lt L. C. Eastman of VFP-63 in an RF-8A – the first F-8 kill by a MiG and the only RF-8 shot down by a MiG during the entire war. Both pilots are captured.

**July 14**  Cdr Dick Bellinger, CO of VF-162, is shot down by a MiG-17 – the second F-8 kill by a MiG.

**September 5**  Four MiG-17s of the 923rd FR bounce F-8s from VF-111 and shoot down USAF exchange pilot Capt W. K. Abbott, who is captured. This is the third, and last, F-8 definitely destroyed by VPAF MiGs, and the third of four confirmed MiG kills over Crusaders in Vietnam.

## 1967

**May 1 and 19**  On these dates eight MiG-17s are downed without loss by F-8s from VF-24 and VF-211. Both squadrons are embarked in USS *Bon Homme Richard* (CVA-31) as part of Carrier Air Wing (CVW) 21.

**December 14**  A lengthy engagement between F-8s of VF-111 and VF-162 and a flight of MiG-17s results in the downing of a MiG-17 by VF-162's Lt Dick Wyman.

## 1968

**June 26**  Lt Cdr L. R. Myers of VF-51 downs a MiG-17.

**July 9**  Lt Cdr John Nichols of VF-191 also shoots down a MiG-17.

**July 29**  Lt Cdr Guy Cane of VF-53 makes the last confirmed MiG-17 kill by an F-8.

## 1972

**May 23**  An unofficial MiG-17 kill by VF-211's Lt Jerry Tucker comes when the VPAF pilot ejects, floating down while the F-8 circles around him. His aircraft carrier, USS *Hancock* (CVA-19), receives credit for the kill, however.

Groundcrews push their MiG-17Fs onto the ramp possibly at Noi Bai. (via Dr István Toperczer)

# DESIGN AND DEVELOPMENT

## F-8 CRUSADER

Towards the end of the Korean War in 1953, the United States started developing a new generation of aircraft. Although the USAF's swept-winged F-86 Sabre had performed relatively well against the MiG-15, the Soviet jet was a dangerous, eye-opening surprise for Allied aviators. The US Navy and US Marine Corps had employed two jet fighters against the MiG, namely the Grumman F9F-2/5 Panther and the twin-engined McDonnell F2H Banshee. Both were straight-winged designs with somewhat low-thrust engines. There were three other USAF jet fighters in Korea, the Republic F-84 Thunderjet, the Lockheed F-80 Shooting Star and the F-94B Starfire, which saw limited service as a nightfighter over Korea (it was derived from the F-80/T-33). All three were straight-winged, as was the US Marine Corps' Douglas F3D Skynight, which, like the F-94B, was a specialist nocturnal hunter. Indeed, it destroyed six communist aircraft while performing this mission, including no fewer than four MiG-15s.

Incorporating new advances in aerodynamics, including the "coke-bottle" pinching of the fuselage that eased transonic flight, post-war fighters in the so-called Century series for the USAF (F-100 through F-106) heralded a new and exciting family of fast and highly capable interceptors for the late 1950s.

Despite the fact that in World War II the F4U Corsair and F6F Hellcat racked up admirable lists of kills, there was a persistent belief (or established axiom) that carrier-based aircraft could not outperform shore-based aircraft. US Navy aircraft required heavier parts such as landing and arresting gear, plus flotation devices and the need for more fuel to fly over large expanses of water. This was all about to change in September 1952 when the US Navy issued a requirement for an advanced carrier fighter. The Bureau of Aeronautics (BuAer) made the request to McDonnell, North American, Douglas, Convair, Lockheed, Grumman, Republic and Vought. Grumman had produced such historic types as the F4F Wildcat and F6F Hellcat and Vought that masterpiece of prop-driven aggression, the F4U Corsair. Finally, Douglas had built one of the icons of the Pacific air war, the SBD Dauntless dive-bomber.

The US Navy wanted a fighter capable of Mach 1.2 at 30,000ft and Mach 0.9 at sea level. It also had to boast a 25,000ft-per-minute rate of climb, coupled with high maneuverability. And all this with a 100-knot landing speed, not to mention the usual shipboard amenities such as folding wings, ease of handling on the flightdeck, and the normal catapult and arresting gear. Armament would include machine guns or cannon, as well as missiles.

Although on paper this looked to be a pretty tall order, Vought filled it. In May 1953 the US Navy chose Vought Model V-383, ordering several mockups and wind-tunnel test models, with the designation XF8U-1. Another model was designated V-392, eventually to become the F8U-1P (later RF-8A) reconnaissance version of the Crusader.

The truly innovative feature of the new Vought fighter was its shoulder-mounted wing, which could be raised seven degrees during takeoffs and landings, providing a variable incidence capability for better visibility in the tricky carrier approach. The view over the nose had never been a Vought trademark, the F4U being a prime example, and many pilots were uncomfortable with the 20-degree angle of attack (AoA) of the infamous F7U Cutlass – carrier approaches are flown by units of AoA, and from their earliest days US Navy pilots are trained in this manner. Vought attempted to retain the necessary AoA by keeping the wing at the required angle, but allowing the fuselage and the cockpit to be lowered for better pilot visibility. Moreover, the aircraft's landing gear could remain at a reasonable weight-saving length.

Vought Chief Test Pilot John W. Konrad poses with XF8U-1 BuNo 138899 in 1955. A one-time bomber pilot, Konrad flew most of Vought's jet aircraft on their first flights. (Vought)

Rear Adm Thomas C. Irwin, who flew one of the earliest Vietnam F-8 deployments with VF-24 aboard USS *Hancock* (CVA-19), described how early Crusader pilots operated the unique wing:

There were two controls in the cockpit – one was the positioning handle and the other a locking handle. After the locking handle was moved to the unlocked or aft position, the positioning handle was moved aft after first depressing a thumb switch on the end. An emergency pneumatic means of activation was available in case of a hydraulic failure.

The extension of the full-span leading edge was also made to the landing position, as well as lowering the narrow inboard flap segments and ailerons. The speed brake also retracted, if extended, and an automatic re-trim of the Unit Horizontal Tail occurred. This was the normal landing configuration. When the wing was lowered, all surfaces returned to the position selected for the cruise droop on the throttle handle.

An ordnanceman loads the cannons of an F-8E during *Oriskany's* 1965 combat cruise. (US Navy)

F-8E Crusader BuNo 150300 was the 108th of 286 "Echo" models manufactured. It is shown as it appeared on June 21, 1966, carrying two AIM-9D Sidewinders, and flown by VF-211's Lt(jg) Phillip V. Vampatella when he scored a kill against a MiG-17 of the VPAF's 923rd FR during a multi-faceted engagement. Damaged by AAA during this action, BuNo 150300 subsequently had its horizontal stabilator repaired in Japan prior to the jet being transferred to the "Hunters" of VF-162, embarked in *Oriskany*. On August 18, 1966, little more than two months after its MiG kill, the fighter was shot down by enemy flak while bearing the side number AH 211. Its pilot, Lt Cdr D. A. "Butch" Verich, was rescued.

For new F-8 pilots, lowering the wing after takeoff was always an interesting experience. Since the wing was doing the flying, aerodynamically the fuselage was raised, and during the auto re-trim the pilot had to *fly* the fuselage up into the wing. To begin transition, procedures called for a speed higher than most pilots were comfortable with. Too little back pressure and the aircraft would settle, too much back pressure and the fighter would climb or porpoise. The correct way was a perfectly level and steady transition to the end of the runway. Formation transitions were also interesting, especially in instrument conditions. Standardized signals alerted the wingman and indicated transition execution. If the wingman failed to anticipate a configuration change, or missed the execute signal, the result was vertical separation and a red face. Landing with the wing down was possible ashore, but risky aboard ship, The approach speed had to be increased some 30 knots, even with the landing droops available, to avoid touching down tailpipe first.

The Crusader enjoyed the advantage of lightweight materials, namely titanium and the Vought-created Metallite. Newly developed aerodynamics also played a large part in the new fighter's design and construction – mainly the area-rule fuselage, the "Coke bottle" pinch of the waist, producing a reduction in drag that increased speeds eventually obtained by the XF8U-1 and all jet fighters that followed.

Another unique feature was the ram air turbine (RAT) installed on a hinged panel in the right side of the forward fuselage that "fell out" into the slip stream to provide emergency electrical and hydraulic power. During the Crusader's long career the RAT saved many an F-8.

The fighter's basic armament was four Colt Mk 12 20mm cannon, two on each side of the forward fuselage, with 144 rounds per gun. Until the later arrival of the

# F-8E CRUSADER

54ft 6in.

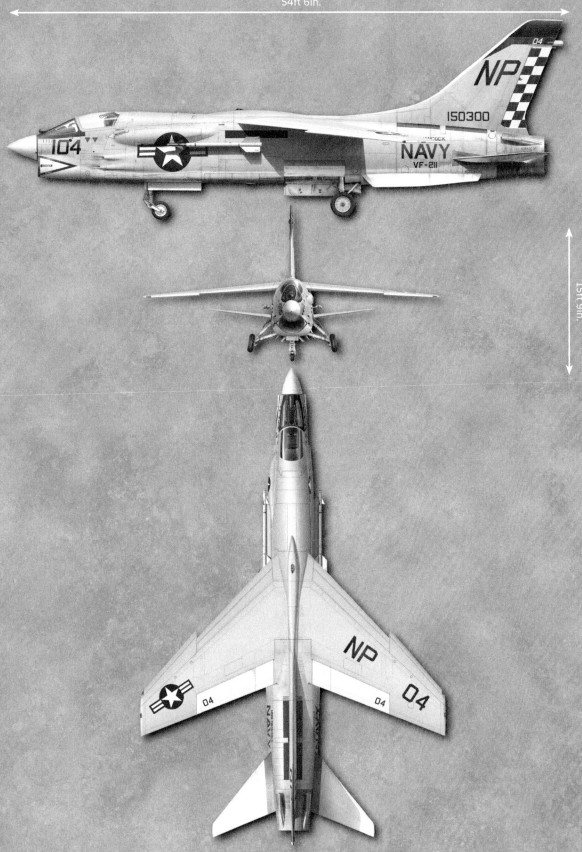

15ft 9in.

35ft 8in.

Grumman F-14 Tomcat (armed with a single 20mm cannon in the nose), this was the last American fighter fitted with internally mounted guns. The USAF's F-4C, basically similar to the US Navy's F-4B, was also devoid of internal armament. The USAF's F-4E boasted a single nose-mounted cannon. The US Navy, US Marine Corps and USAF experimented with "gun packs" (externally mounted pods with one or two guns, sometimes cannon), and Air Force Phantom II crews scored a few kills with these pods. The USAF's F-105 Thunderchief, originally designed as a nuclear-armed fighter-bomber, was fitted with a single 20mm nose cannon.

The first F-8As were equipped with a belly-mounted rocket pack (eliminated in later models). This was the beginning of the time of the missile-armed fighter. With major advances in small, ostensibly highly capable air-to-air missiles (AAMs), the US Department of Defense decided that the day of the solely gun-armed fighter was gone. Dogfighting and skilful shooting had had their day, and in the coming generations of fighters the missile that could now be fired two miles from the target was the way to go. It sounded good, but the early AIM-7 Sparrows and AIM-9 Sidewinders that hung off F-4s and F-8s all too often, when most needed, did not work. In the first years of the war in Vietnam the kill ratio between US and North Vietnamese fighters reflected the unreliability of American AAMs. This would change with vast improvements in missile operation, as witness the F-8's first combat encounters when, although the usual load was two AIM-9s due to weight and fuel considerations, the fighter could carry as many as four Sidewinders.

The XF8U-1 (BuNo 138899) used a Pratt & Whitney J57-P-11 turbojet that delivered 14,800lbs of thrust in afterburner, giving the new fighter outstanding performance of nearly 700mph at 1,000ft and more than 1,100mph at 35,000ft. The J57's ratings increased throughout the Crusader's career, and until it was retired in the late 1980s it was one of the fleet's fastest, most maneuverable aircraft. The RF-8 photo-reconnaissance variant, which carried enough internal fuel for an entire sortie, frequently outran its F-4 escorts, who usually had to seek a tanker. The XF8U-1's maiden flight occurred on March 25, 1955, with Vought chief test pilot John W. Konrad at the controls. He easily passed Mach 1, the prototype Crusader thus becoming the first US Navy fighter to achieve this in level flight.

The first production F8U-1 left the Dallas plant on September 20, 1955, and the US Marine Corps duly accepted its first production Crusader in January 1956. Fleet introduction began shortly thereafter as the first cadre of pilots commenced training on their new fighter at Naval Air Station (NAS) Patuxent River, Maryland. VF-32 at NAS Cecil Field, Florida, accepted the first fleet Crusaders, and for the Pacific Fleet the first examples went to VF(AW)-3.

When the basic F-8 fighter was modified to accommodate a suite of reconnaissance cameras the second Crusader was born. The F8U-1P (RF-8A, later RF-8G) served both the US Navy and the US Marine Corps, beginning its career in October 1962 in the Cuban Missile Crisis. In Operation *Blue Moon*, detailed, real-time photographs by RF-8 pilots of VFP-62 and US Marine Corps squadron VMCJ-2 proved the existence in Cuba of Soviet intermediate range missiles capable of reaching the eastern US.

By mid-1963 the F-8 was serving aboard carriers large and small, and on the frontline of what would soon become a real war in Southeast Asia.

# MiG-17

By far the VPAF fighter most frequently encountered by American flight crews over the skies of North Vietnam was the MiG-17. Although possessing a number of earlier MiG-15UTI two-seat trainers and more modern MiG-19 and MiG-21 fighters, the VPAF favored the MiG-17 (codenamed "Fresco"). The North Vietnamese fighters came from the Soviet manufacturer MiG (an acronym of the names of the two men who designed the aircraft, Artem Mikoyan and Mikhail Gurevich). That brilliant little Korean War performer, the MiG-15, was not the company's first jet fighter, that honor belonging to the 1949-50 Soviet Air Force MiG-9 (a few of which were presented to communist China as its first jet fighters). The MiG design bureau soon developed the MiG-15, which debuted in the late 1940s to an indifferent Western opinion.

When the silver jet first tangled with American fighters over Korea in late 1950, there was a rude awakening. The MiG was fast, with a higher service ceiling than Western fighters, and its three heavy nose-mounted cannon packed a mighty punch. An added insult was that many Korean MiG-15s were flown by Soviet "volunteers" with combat experience from World War II – it was hard to disguise the large, sometimes fair-haired men in the cockpits speaking whirlwind Russian in the heat of battle! The MiG-15, and its clearly demonstrated capabilities, was as lethal a surprise to the Americans of Korea as the Japanese Mitsubishi A6M Zero-sen had been to their elders in World War II. The sleek new high-tailed heavily armed MiG-15, when flown properly, was the measure of any Western fighter.

MiG was already at work on the MiG-17, a major redesign of the MiG-15. The new fighter featured a lengthened (by nearly three feet) rear fuselage and a new wing. The MiG-17 retained the VK-1F engine that had powered later model MiG-15s, as well as the aircraft's three-cannon (two 23mm and one 37mm) armament. The first production MiG-17s ("Fresco-As") entered service with the Soviet Air Forces in 1952. Later improvements resulted in the "Fresco-B" through "D", with the "C" and "D" featuring an afterburning VK-1F and, in the "D", a small nose-mounted air-to-air radar (an instant recognition feature with its protruding fairing to house the radar). The VPAF soon flew a number of MiG-17F "Fresco-Cs", and it was this particular airplane that bore the brunt

The entire aft section of the MiG-17's fuselage could be pulled off, thus providing easy access to the engine, and its accessories. The VK-1 was a single-spool turbojet with a centrifugal compressor. The version fitted to the MiG-17 boasted an afterburner, which produced about 25 percent more thrust. (via Dr István Toperczer)

Groundcrews ready four MiG-17s at Noi Bai. Two technicians are manhandling an engine starter cart across the apron to a waiting fighter out of shot. No. 3012 wears a very weathered dark green paint scheme, while 2031 and 2041 are painted in gray overall. Only 2056, furthest from the camera, is in natural metal. (via Dr István Toperczer)

MiG-17F 2310 was flown by Capt Pham Ngoc Lan of the 923rd FR, based at Noi Bai, on April 3, 1965 during the first engagement between VPAF fighters and F-8 Crusaders. Having erroneously claimed to have downed the aircraft flown by VF-211's Lt Cdr Spence Thomas, Pham Ngoc Lan failed to make it back to base due to fuel starvation. He had to crash-land this jet on the banks of the Duong River, where he was helped by local villagers. 2310 was repaired and returned to flight status, participating in several other aerial actions until it was retired to a flying school to be studied by students.

of aerial combat against US Navy F-8s. Unsurprisingly, therefore, it was also the airplane that accounted for the majority of American kills from the spring of 1965 through to January 1973 (see the table that lists MiG kills by US flight crews in Chapter 6).

The first official F-8 kill occurred on June 12, 1966, while the last official F-8 kill, albeit a MiG-21, came on September 9, 1968. In little more than two years, the Crusader scored 16 MiG-17 victories (including the second for Hal Marr, which is not officially recognized by the US Navy despite the VPAF acknowledging it). With the three officially recognized (by the US) kills by MiG-17s over F-8s, plus one RF-8 (Lt Eastman on June 21, 1966), along with four MiG-21 F-8 kills, Crusader pilots enjoyed a 20-to-4 (or five-to-one) kill rate. Given the small number of MiG-17s available to the VPAF, and how rarely their valuable fighters were sent against large US strike packages, the F-8's kill-to-loss ratio is quite good.

Other American types – US Navy, US Marine Corps and USAF F-4s and USAF F-105s – may have scored more MiG-17 kills, but the Thunderchief and later USAF Phantom IIs carried one internal 20mm cannon and a good number of air-to-air missiles. The F-8 carried four cannon, which, especially in turning engagements, were less than dependable, and early AIM-9 Sidewinder missiles. As previously noted, these were equally undependable. To make one kill, frustrated Crusader drivers frequently had to shoot two and sometimes three of the $100,000 missiles.

A two-tour American aviator's greater flight hour experience, coupled with the Crusader's top speed (twice that of the MiG-17), could offset the MiG's maneuverability and the punch of its three heavy cannon. Like in Korea, there were also reported instances of other nationalities flying the MiGs. Actually, through an agreement between Hanoi and Pyongyang (according to a very recent VPAF publication), only volunteer North Korean pilots flew in combat for the North Vietnamese. These aviators served exclusively with the 923rd FR, in the so-called "Z" Squadron. Soviet advisors only flew on training flights in the two-seat MiG-21UM trainer, which was unarmed. No other nationalities were involved. The North Koreans were especially active during the summer of 1967, with at least three of them being shot down by F-8s – as many as 12 North Korean MiG-17 pilots may have died during the war.

# MiG-17F "FRESCO-C"

36ft 5in.

12ft 5in.

31ft 7in.

# TECHNICAL SPECIFICATIONS

## F-8 CRUSADER

Two Crusader fighter types bore the brunt of the action in Vietnam, namely the F-8C and F-8E. The F-8D also saw combat in the first year of the conflict following the Gulf of Tonkin Incident in August 1964, with VF-111 and VF-154 being embarked aboard USS *Midway* (CVA-41) and USS *Coral Sea* (CVA-43), respectively. The "Charlie" and "Echo" flew from the so-called "27-Charlie" carriers (named for a series of modifications to existing World War II *Essex*-class ships), USS *Intrepid* (CVA/S-11), USS *Ticonderoga* (CVA-14), USS *Hancock* (CVA-19), USS *Oriskany* (CVA-34) and USS *Shangri-la* (CVA/S-38).

The unarmed photo-reconnaissance RF-8A/G flew from both the "27-Charlies" and the larger decks carriers *Midway*, *Coral Sea* and USS *Franklin D. Roosevelt* (CVA-42). The RF-8s were also embarked, on a rotating basis, in USS *Ranger* (CVA-61), USS *Kitty Hawk* (CVA-63) and USS *Constellation* (CVA-64) during the early stages of the conflict, although they were soon replaced by the more sophisticated (if not as dependable) RA-5C Vigilantes.

This volume focuses on the exploits of the "Charlie", "Delta" and "Echo" model Crusaders. Initially designated the F8U (denoting that it was the eighth fighter design by Vought), subsequent Crusader models carried letters – i.e. the F8U-2N, or

Photographed on February 7, 1965, CVW-21 aircraft embarked in *Hancock* prepare to launch on the US Navy's first Alpha strike of the Vietnam conflict. Behind the VA-212 A-4E, two VF-24 F-8Cs wait their turn to move up to the catapults. Lt Cdr Greg Gregory is at the controls of NP 440 while Lt(jg) Tom Irwin is strapped into NP 450. Both F-8s carry two AIM-9Bs. (via T. C. Irwin)

F8U-2NE. The burgeoning numbering system proved too cumbersome, and in October 1962 it was changed to denote specific aircraft. The F8U-1E became the F-8B, the F8U-2N the F-8C and the F8U-2NE the F-8E. It took time to accept the new system, and older aviators can still be heard referring to their time in the "F8U" or, more directly, "the Deuce", meaning the F8U-2, or post-1962, the F-8C.

The first production model, the F8U-1 (F-8A) was fitted with four Colt 20mm cannon in the lower forward fuselage area. "Y pylons" that enabled the fuselage stations for F-8Cs to carry four Sidewinders did not arrive until 1965. Adm Irwin, who as a "jaygee" had flown with VF-24 aboard *Hancock* during its early 1965 deployment, commented, "Once we got them [the Y pylons] we always carried four".

Initially included in the F-8's armament was a unique battery of 32 Mighty Mouse 2.75-in. folding fin aerial rockets (FFARs) in eight tubes in a compartment in the belly below the cockpit, supposedly providing the fighter with more ground-attack capability. However, when the Crusader began carrying heavier bombs the FFARs were deleted in order to save weight. The Y pylons could also carry two pods on each side, with one 5-in. Zuni rocket per pod – it could be four pods instead of any Sidewinders, or a rare combination of one AIM-9 and one Zuni pod on each pylon. The Zunis gave the aircraft a hefty and useful punch when attacking trucks and trains.

The Crusader had problems with its guns – namely too wide a dispersion of bullets. The Colt Mk 12 fired 600 rounds per minute, which gave the pilot just 13 seconds of sustained fire. With the eventual addition of electronic countermeasures (ECM) gear in the nose, the F-8 series lacked sufficient expansion space for more ammunition. In high-g maneuvers pilots experienced ammunition jams, which was a cause for concern while ground strafing. A partial solution came from VF-124, the Crusader training squadron at NAS Miramar in San Diego. The unit rewired the gun circuitry and installed two switches in the cockpit that duly allowed the pilot to select which pair of guns to fire, thereby conserving his ammunition.

Missile wiring and switchology was also an occasional concern. A-4 pilots on Alpha strikes (large air wing bombing missions) dreaded the call "Fox away!" from the F-8 escorts above them as this signified an AIM-9, inadvertently fired, was loose among the bombers. This usually happened when, as the strike package went feet dry and headed inland toward the target, F-8 pilots turned on their "Master Arm" switches and stray voltage fired a Sidewinder.

The F-8B (F8U-1E) replaced the F8U-1's APG-30 fire control radar with the AN/APS-67, giving the "Bravo" limited all-weather capability. The B-model also retained the "Alpha's" ventrally mounted rocket pack, although most squadrons sealed it off and never used it.

The first true fleet Crusader fighter was the F-8C, which flew in August 1957 as the F8U-2. Among other improvements over previous models, the "Charlie" had a new engine, the Pratt & Whitney J57-P-16 – 13,000lb of thrust in basic engine and 17,500lb in afterburner, which was 1000lb more than in earlier engines. F-8 performance increased, as did the afterburner's temperature. To help cool the aircraft's aft section, two air scoops were mounted on the F-8C's tail cone, and ventral strakes were added to the rear fuselage for increased directional stability at high altitudes. The "Charlie" also added two more Sidewinder rails to its fuselage racks, although the four-missile armament was only occasionally carried in combat. Pilots considered the weight penalty and reduction in fuel load not worth the extra missiles. Some squadrons like VF-24 and VF-162 appear to have used the four-Sidewinder load more than others, however.

The F8U-2N followed as a development of the F-8C, duly designated the F-8D. Believed by many pilots to be the fastest of the Crusader line thanks to its powerful J57-P-20 engine (18,000lb of thrust in afterburner), it served with only two US Navy squadrons in combat, VF-111 and VF-154. Intended as a nightfighter, the "Delta" featured improved radar and avionics, and the addition of the approach power compensator, but finally eliminated the ventral rocket pack.

The next Crusader, and most produced model (and the last production F-8) was the F8U-2NE or F-8E, which was also the top MiG killer (11 victories). The "Echo" added two underwing pylons and saw considerable action as a ground-attack weapon. Indeed, at one time it was the only fighter capable of carrying Mk 84 2,000lb bombs, one under each wing. The F-8E could also fire the Bullpup air-to-ground missile, which was rarely used by US Marine Corps Crusaders (although often by US Navy A-4s). The F-8E served with all US Marine Corps squadrons in Vietnam, and it was used to great advantage as a weapon, often delivering ordnance directly ahead of Marine ground units surrounded by enemy troops.

With the growing intensity of the Vietnam War, the US Navy decided to keep many of the aging, smaller, "27C" carriers in operation. Normal attrition and heavy combat, where ground fire and a few MiG kills had downed several F-8s, reduced the number of available Crusaders. The Vought Aeronautics Division of the now-renamed Ling-Temco-Vought (LTV) company, was tasked with refurbishing existing airframes, reconditioning them and, in many cases, re-equipping older F-8s with current avionics suites. The letters G through L (with the letter "I" omitted) were allotted for these remanufactured F-8s.

The most significant modifications to all models were the fitting of a wing with a service life of 4,000 hours and a longer nose landing-gear strut. Two inches longer

## F-8E GUNS AND MISSILES

The F-8 was the only US Navy fighter that included internal guns and external missiles as its air-to-air weapons suite. The original design carried four 20mm Colt Mk 12 cannon. The AIM-9B Sidewinder was added to the F8U-2 (F-8C), with two missiles, one on each side on external racks below the cockpit. The Zuni 5-in. air-to-ground rocket gave further depth to the Crusader's armoury, and although not truly an air-to-air weapon, a few pilots tried their hand with the big rocket when dueling with MiGs. Single Zunis could be carried on individual Sidewinder rails, but the LAU-10 rocket pod held four Zunis, allowing four to eight rockets per F-8.

When the pilot selected Master Arm Switch "On" and squeezed the trigger switch halfway on the control column in the cockpit it opened the gun vent doors on the underside of the forward fuselage. The smaller forward door allowed air to be "rammed" into the gun bay when the weapons were fired, forcing both it and collected gas out through the larger, rearward-facing doors.

The aluminum ammunition boxes were designed specifically for the F-8 and carried 110 to 125 rounds of high-explosive armor-piercing 20mm cannon shells, with every fifth round being a tracer. The cannons occasionally jammed, especially during turns in excess of 3.5G, much to the frustration of the pilots bent on killing a MiG. The low ammunition capacity was solved in part by allowing pilots to select upper or lower pairs of the guns, which, while decreasing the number of shells being fired, increased the firing time. The F-8C gained increased firepower with the arrival of the four-station "Y" racks that could carry either Sidewinders or Zunis, and occasionally, a mix. The Zunis could be preset to fire singly, or in a ripple pattern with 0.1 seconds between each rocket. The "Bravo" Sidewinder weighed 167lb and the "Delta" 198lb. The warheads were, respectively, ten pounds or twenty pounds of high-explosive. The "Delta's" range had increased to two miles over the "Bravo's" 1.2 miles.

The F-8 used three types of Sidewinder during the war – the AIM-9B (IR seeker head), the AIM-9D (semi-active radar IR head) and the rarely carried, trouble prone, AIM-9C (semi-active radar-guided head), designed specifically for the Crusader. A surplus of "Bravos" early in the war required many squadrons to call for "Deltas" to be ferried over from other carriers when MiGs were expected in upcoming missions than the original struts, the latter could absorb ten per cent more energy. All modified aircraft would also receive stronger main gear.

Another major addition was the Boundary Layer Control (BLC) in the F-8J, which was a remanufactured "Echo". BLC, which first appeared in the 42 F-8E(FN)s purchased by the French Navy, provided additional lift during takeoff and landing by routing engine bleed air over the uppersurface of the flaps and ailerons, permitting the aircraft to be flown slower and thus improving its performance around the carrier. An extensive change, the BLC required internal ducting, a reduction in angle of incidence of the wing and a larger UHT (unit horizontal tail) for adequate longitudinal control at the lower landing speeds. The BLC met with mixed success, and to this day F-8 veterans question its value. Recent, and often involved, discussion on the very active Crusader website contain such comments. I provide them in full here to show the reader how difficult it was at times to have satisfactory changes made, or unsatisfactory modifications deleted.

According to P. J. Smith, "the difference was the continued addition of ECM, which everyone agreed at the time was needed ASAP. Continued addition of weight caused changes in wing-incident angle, leading edge changes, larger UHT, etc. as the weight of the F-8J went up well above the basic F-8E(FN). The French bird never had that problem. And I never stated that PAX [NAS Patuxent] River signed off on the F-8J. They did highly recommend the BLC system as a way to reduce F-8 approach speed dramatically, which was absolutely true".

Kurt Schroeder was also involved in the BLC debate. "I can probably provide some insight into the F-8J discussion regarding 'How can something like this reach the fleet?' Assigned to the Carrier Suitability Branch at PAX when the F-8J appeared, I was not initially involved because I was knee-deep with the British F-4K project. The F-8J Project Pilot was Sidney 'Kent' Billue, a highly qualified fleet-experienced Crusader pilot. The F-8J was the promised solution to all of the Crusader approach challenges, plus providing reduced wind-over-deck requirements for the 27C decks. NAVAIR [Naval Air Systems Command] pointed to the excellent carrier approach safety record of the A-6, and gave much too much credit to the single characteristic of low approach speed. Many of the F-8Es were getting 'long-in-the-tooth', and the prospect of getting a re-manufactured 'better-than-new' airframe was highly anticipated. Unfortunately, introduction of the airplane was way behind schedule, and the fleet was howling for it.

"I remember talking to 'Kent' after his first hop in the airplane, and his immediate concern was the lack of excess thrust in the BLC ON approach configuration. Why this wasn't addressed during the LTV development of the airplane remains a mystery because with a significant gross weight/induced drag increase, plus a reduction in available engine thrust, the consequences should have been obvious.

"As the carrier-suitability test program proceeded, 'Kent' advised NAVAIR that until the wave-off performance of the airplane was improved, the airplane was UNSUITABLE for fleet use. NAVAIR was getting enormous pressure from the operational side of the house to release the airplane, and 'Kent's' prediction of numerous ramp strikes went unheeded. I still remember the Landing Signal Officer's comment on an F-8J ramp strike – 'nothing is more terrifying to an LSO than to give an F-8J a wave-off and see nothing change but the quantity of black smoke out the back'. I was astounded when I had the chance to fly the airplane in the landing pattern. You could choose to turn downwind or to climb to pattern altitude, but not at the same time. The fleet was its own worst enemy, as illustrated by a message released by an F-8J skipper stating he had initiated a wave-off two feet above the deck and never touched down'.

"NAVAIR ignored the NATC [Naval Air Test Center] recommendation and released the airplane. 'Kent's' prediction of ramp strikes proved to be correct, and a program was initiated to address the problem. 'Kent' had moved over to the TPS staff by then, and the test program to evaluate AFC-544 (reduction in flap/aileron deflection to decrease drag, plus restrictors to reduce BLC bleed air flow) and the engine upgrade to the J57-P-420 fell in my lap.

"The BLC ON approach speed increased by 2-3 knots, but everything else moved in the right direction. Altitude loss following a wave-off holding on-speed AoA did not change significantly, but this was a consequence of F-8 characteristics – a flat thrust vector and shallow thrust required curve. A recommendation to rotate slightly took advantage of the improved

acceleration/climb profile, and instead of just decelerating, the modified airplane performed much better. The APCS [Approach Power Compensator System] performance was also improved through incorporation of UHT input and higher gains. When APCS was first introduced in the F-8, its ability to reduce the likelihood of a decelerating approach was important, but like all APCSs at that time, it needed to see an error in order to command a power change. The addition of UHT input provided a 'lead term' in that, like the pilot, an aft stick correction was accompanied by a power addition, and vice versa for a forward stick input.

"Optimizing the APCS for all pilots was an impossible task, for 'smooth' pilots preferred a high gain system, while pilots that 'stirred-the-pot' objected to the throttles 'dancing around'. At the Carrier Suitability Branch we always favored the higher gains because, with experience, pilots could adapt to it, while the 'smooth pilot' could never be happy with a low gain system.

"The F-8J remained a demanding airplane for the carrier landing task, but the modified airplane represented about as much as could be wrung out of it. The real solution of the F-8 approach task was Direct Lift Control (DLC). The Carrier

Lt(jg) Henry Livingston of VF-211 goes through his pre-start checks before launching from *Hancock* in 1972. His F-8J is armed with two Sidewinders, as well as the Crusader's internal 20mm cannon. (via Henry Livingston)

23

An F-8H of VF-51 is directed onto the catapult aboard *Bon Homme Richard* in 1968. The "Screaming Eagles" were credited with two MiG-21 victories during this cruise – the only victories attributed to the H-model Crusader. (US Navy)

Suitability Branch had an F-8C modified with the system, and I had the opportunity to take it to a West Coast 27C. All of the adverse carrier approach configuration characteristics of the F-8 design were masked by the DLC. After flying the ball onto the mirror, all glide slope corrections could be made through the DLC thumbwheel. Aircraft glide slope response was instantaneous, making even a 'low in close' an easy correction. The APCS referenced airspeed vice AoA, and normal glide slope inputs were not complicated by bursts of power. Unfortunately, DLC didn't offer the operational benefit of reduced wind-over-deck for the 27Cs, and once reported to be part of the F-8H configuration, it died a quiet death. This was probably a good thing because had DLC-equipped F-8Hs hit the fleet, Crusader pilots would have been offering up their 'first-borns' for orders to an 'H' squadron."

The F-8J was later fitted with the bigger J57-P-420 engine, which relieved the problems of low power in the landing pattern. The F-8H included underwing pylons and Bullpup missile control systems. A sub-variant of the "Hotel" was the F-8P, 35 of which were sold to the Philippines in 1977.

Henry Livingston, a lieutenant "jaygee" with VF-211 aboard *Hancock* during 1971-72, offers his memories of the F-8J:

One of the factors that led to ramp strikes with the newly "BLC'd" J57-P-20-powered F-8J was that the tests on it were done in the colder, less humid air of the US west and east coasts. The higher humidity and heat in the Tonkin Gulf further reduced already marginal wave off end thrust. VF-211 had several ramp strikes during this period. We lost Guido Carloni at night off Hawaii on a ramp strike, and John Bodanske hit the ramp in the Tonkin Gulf during the day but ejected successfully. Rick Amber's day ramp strike and ejection resulted in near fatal injuries that paralyzed him for the rest of his life.

During my time, there were two big changes to F-8J pilot safety. The first was the introduction of the Martin-Baker Mk 7 ejection seat, which gave us a zero-zero capability – zero ground speed and zero altitude for a minimum ejection. A pilot still had to have at least 600ft to survive an inverted ejection at zero sink rate.

The second big change was the retrofit of the "Juliet" with a J57-P-420 engine. The added thrust and other aerodynamic changes improved survivability in the Tonkin Gulf, and thereafter few ramp strikes occurred because of a lack of "dirty" thrust or poor wave off capability.

After remanufacturing, 61 F-8Bs were re-designated as F-8Ls. Some 87 F-8Cs were also refurbished as F-8Ks and mainly flown by US Marine Corps Reserve squadrons and US Navy utility units. A total of 89 F-8Ds were converted into F-8Hs and 136 F-8Es into F-8Js. Finally, 73 RF-8As were rebuilt as RF-8Gs. Many of the newly refurbished Crusaders served with fleet units until US participation in the conflict in Vietnam came to an end in early 1973, after which they were assigned to Naval Air Reserve squadrons until supplanted by F-4B Phantom IIs. The photo-reconnaissance Crusaders also found second homes in the reserves, with the last US Navy RF-8 squadrons, VFP-206 and VFP-306, not being decommissioned until 1987 and 1984, respectively.

# MiG-17 "FRESCO-C"

This was the main production variant of the MiG-17 following limited manufacture of the MiG-17 "Fresco-A". An afterburner was added to the Klimov VK-1F engine, boosting its performance by more than 600lb static thrust. This in turn increased the fighter's service ceiling by 1,000ft and doubled its rate of climb. The "Fresco-C" had hydraulic airbrakes of increased area, which could be deflected to 55 degrees to force an enemy fighter to overshoot in combat.

The wing was an improved version of the MiG-15's, with a thinner aerofoil to increase speed, greater sweep-back and area and three "fences" to control boundary layer air. It contained no fuel tanks, unlike the F-8's wing, making it less vulnerable in combat. The MiG-17F's internal fuel capacity was only 374 gallons, and a further 176 gallons could be carried in two drop tanks. Refueling was by the gravity method via two filler caps behind the cockpit, with a third at the side of the rear fuselage for the 35-gallon tank that was located beneath the engine exhaust pipe.

In all respects the maintenance of the aircraft was very simple, using basic tools and lubricant cans. The single hydraulic system powered the landing gear, flaps, airbrakes and aileron actuating mechanism. Two pneumatic systems actuated the wheel brakes, pressurised the cockpit and charged the guns, as well as providing a back-up system to lower the undercarriage and flaps. The entire rear section of the fuselage could be detached at a point just forward of the wing trailing edge, allowing full access for engine maintenance.

The forward fuselage section, which was very similar to the MiG-15's, contained the pressurised cockpit, two avionics bays, the No 1 fuel tank and a weapons bay.

To simplify re-arming and maintenance of the MiG-17's guns, the three cannon, their ammunition boxes and pneumatic charging mechanisms were built into a tray that could be lowered from the fuselage by its own built-in winch. Simple refueling methods and this "palletized" gun system meant that the aircraft could be turned around in 20 minutes and sent back into action.

A pilot boards his MiG-17 "Fresco-A" (almost certainly a Chinese-built Shenyang J-5) using a short ladder. The circular port above the main intake is the fighter's gun camera, a similar device being seen in this location on the MiG-15 and MiG-19. (via Dr István Toperczer)

The Nudel'man N-37D 37mm cannon had been in Soviet service since 1946. Designed for bomber interceptors, it could fire 400 massive rounds per minute, although no more than 40 were normally carried. It developed powerful recoil action, which was used to recharge the gun, and the weapon's waste gases, discharged close to the engine intake, could cause the powerplant to surge dangerously. On the left hand side of the gun bay were two Nudel'man-Rikhter NR-23 single-barrel 23mm cannon capable of firing more than 650 rounds per minute, with 80 rounds carried per gun. This weapon was installed in a wide variety of Soviet aircraft and license-manufactured in China.

Together, the three guns could deliver more than 70lb of shells in a two-second burst – twice the weight of fire of the F-8 Crusader's four 20mm cannon. However, gun harmonisation was often inadequate, and a primitive gunsight, together with aircraft vibration and stability problems at high speed, reduced the effect of the slow-firing cannons. US pilots reported many occurrences of inaccurate shooting by MiG-17 pilots, even at close range.

Powering the MiG-17 was an engine that originated in 1944 as the Rolls-Royce Nene, used in the British Sea Hawk and Attacker fighters. The Soviets produced 39,000 unlicensed copies, and it remained in production in China until 1979. Simple and cheap to build, the smokeless Nene (designated the Klimov VK-1F in the USSR) had a single centrifugal compressor and a single-stage axial turbine. Klimov added a short afterburner with a two-position nozzle, although this took more than five seconds to light up and could only be used for three minutes continuously. Engine acceleration was, therefore, generally slow. Despite this, the VK-1F allowed the MiG-17F to maintain a tight turn at lower airspeeds better than US fighters. And although the "Fresco-C" was only marginally faster than the non-afterburning "Fresco-A", its rate of climb, however, was nearly twice that of the original MiG-17.

Vietnam's somewhat temperate climate permitted much of the aircraft maintenance carried out by the VPAF to be performed outside. Here, this well-camouflaged facility shows a "Fresco-C" of the 923rd FR receiving attention under bamboo shelters. Such facilities provided good camouflage against American bombers, for the huts were usually located in villages or agricultural cooperatives, making them difficult to spot from the air. Seeing these conditions, one can easily understand why the VPAF suffered such a high attrition rate with its jet fighters. (via Dr István Toperczer)

Flying controls were conventional ailerons, elevators and a rudder, all operated by mechanical rods and cranks, with electrically operated trim tabs. The lack of powered control augmentation as fitted to US fighters made the controls very heavy to operate, even with the unusually long control column to provide leverage. At 500 knots stability and maneuverability became poor, and it was impossible to pull the nose up to a steep angle. Above 595 knots at altitudes below 16,000ft, the airframe suffered from severe buffeting and the flying controls had little effect.

The undercarriage typified the fighter's manual/mechanical systems. To lower it meant flipping a toggle switch, activating a pump and allowing hydraulic pressure to build up prior to pushing down a handle to lower and lock the undercarriage. The hydraulic pump then had to be switched off.

The pilot's bubble canopy provided better visibility than that of later MiG-21s and many American fighters, although heavy frames, a bulky gunsight and a 2.5-in. thick bulletproof glass windscreen restricted forward vision. Chinese license-built MiG-17Fs were designated Jianjiji-5s, or J-5s – these were also flown in considerable numbers by the VPAF.

The MiG-17 was much lighter than its western adversaries, endowing the Soviet jet with superb maneuverability. Heavier American fighters such as the F-105 and F-4 could not match the smaller MiG in a turn, and with no guns they needed a more specific and advantageous setup before they could fire missiles. The MiG pilot could spray his nose-mounted cannon in a wider fan to more readily hit his target. For all that, like its opponents, the MiG's ammunition was limited. The VPAF pilot had to be miserly when shooting. Moreover, he relied heavily on communications with his ground controller – a basic characteristic of most Soviet fighters.

Like the MiG-15, the "Fresco" was tough and capable of absorbing battle damage. One pilot reported taking as many as seven hits and still being able to return to his base. British author Roger Boniface wrote in *MiGs Over North Vietnam* (Specialty Press, 2008), "The real defect of the MiG-17 during the Vietnam war was the pilot, often inexperienced and often flying into combat to take on the American veterans of the Korean War, and even some from the Second World War". "Defect" notwithstanding, the MiG-17 presented a serious threat to any and all American aircraft, and none more so than to the Naval Aviators flying Crusaders. Many of the 18-20 MiG-17 pilots shot down by F-8s were probably junior aviators, but others were experienced drivers, some of whom had been flying for more than five years, and had trained in the Soviet Union.

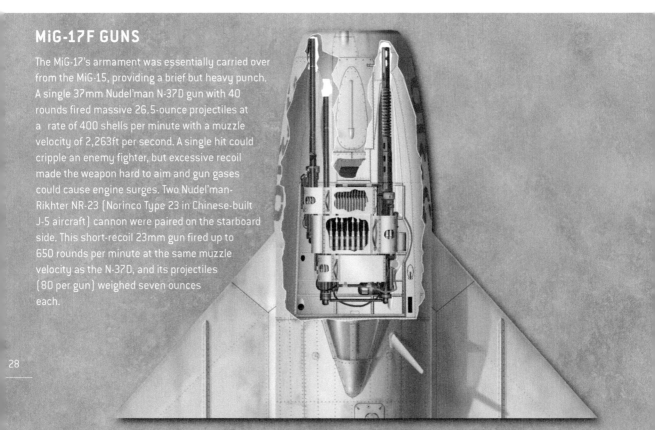

## MiG-17F GUNS

The MiG-17's armament was essentially carried over from the MiG-15, providing a brief but heavy punch. A single 37mm Nudel'man N-37D gun with 40 rounds fired massive 26.5-ounce projectiles at a rate of 400 shells per minute with a muzzle velocity of 2,263ft per second. A single hit could cripple an enemy fighter, but excessive recoil made the weapon hard to aim and gun gases could cause engine surges. Two Nudel'man-Rikhter NR-23 (Norinco Type 23 in Chinese-built J-5 aircraft) cannon were paired on the starboard side. This short-recoil 23mm gun fired up to 650 rounds per minute at the same muzzle velocity as the N-37D, and its projectiles (80 per gun) weighed seven ounces each.

In early March 1965, when US Navy carrier aircraft were committed to Operation *Rolling Thunder*, the VPAF was untried, but ready to contest the skies over North Vietnam with American aviators. Amongst the latter were US Navy F-8 squadrons.

| F-8E Crusader and MiG-17F comparison specifications | | |
|---|---|---|
| | **F-8E Crusader** | **MiG-17F** |
| **Powerplant** | Pratt & Whitney J57-P-20A rated at 18,000lb maximum thrust | one Klimov VK-1F rated at 7,452lb in afterburner |
| | | |
| **Dimensions** | | |
| Wingspan | 35ft 8in. | 31ft 7in. |
| Length | 54ft 6in. | 36ft 5in. |
| Height | 15ft 9in. | 12ft 5in. |
| Wing Area | 375 sq. ft | 243 sq. ft |
| | | |
| **Weights** | | |
| Empty | 17,541lb | 8,664lb |
| Loaded (air combat) | 29,000lb | 13,858lb |
| | | |
| **Performance** | | |
| Max speed | 1,225mph at 36,000ft | 655mph at 38,000ft |
| Range | 450 miles (combat radius) | 646 miles (with two external tanks) |
| Climb | 31,950ft per minute | 12,795ft per minute |
| Service ceiling | 58,000ft | 48,446ft |
| | | |
| Armament (air-to-air) | 4 x Colt Mk 12 20mm cannon 2 x AIM-9D Sidewinders | 1 x N-37D 37mm cannon 2 x NR-23 23mm cannon |

# THE STRATEGIC SITUATION

The Crusader – fighter and photo-reconnaissance aircraft – was in there from the beginning. Trouble in Southeast Asia was not new. US Navy and US Marine Corps squadrons had been operating in the region since World War II, and in March 1961, when civil war broke out in Laos, VMF-154 and VMF-312 with their 34 F8U-1Es (F-8Bs) were sent to the Philippines. In May 1962, as the crisis in Laos continued, eight VMF-451 Crusaders were put aboard *Hancock*. US Navy carriers continued patrolling the waters off the Vietnamese coast, squadrons flying inland training missions and, at the same time, mentoring the small South Vietnamese air force.

While other Crusader-equipped squadrons trained, RF-8 dets (detachments, usually consisting of three aircraft, five or six pilots and 40 enlisted maintenance men) traveled around the Seventh Fleet's carriers. The photo-Crusaders flew combat reconnaissance missions, which made them the first American aircraft to be shot at in this initial phase of what became a major conflict. June 6, 1964 saw the first loss of *any* Crusader in combat when VFP-63's Lt Charles Klusmann of the squadron det aboard *Kitty Hawk* was shot down over Laos. Klusmann spent three months as a prisoner of the Pathet Lao. Along with several Laotian prisoners, he finally escaped, but only after a harrowing experience where his fellow prisoners were killed. Klusmann's story foretold the fate of all too many American PoWs in the oncoming Vietnam War.

A bloody coup that toppled the government of South Vietnam's President Ngo Dinh Diem on November 1, 1963 set the stage for what was to come. Following the assassination three weeks later of US President John F. Kennedy, his successor, Lyndon

Johnson, increased the already substantial presence in Vietnam of American advisors and troops. And then on the afternoon of August 2, 1964, in the Gulf of Tonkin, the North Vietnamese sent three PT boats to harass a force of American destroyers supporting a South Vietnamese military operation. Several F-8 squadrons were on hand.

Many readers will be familiar with the events in the Tonkin Gulf on August 2 and 4. There was one definite attack by three communist PT boats in the mid-afternoon of August 2. The enemy vessels struck USS *Maddox* (DD-731), which returned fire, damaging all three attackers. The carrier *Ticonderoga* sent in a patrol of F-8Es from VF-51 and VF-53, led by VF-51 CO Cdr James B. Stockdale (later to gain honor and fame as a PoW). Stockdale fired Zuni rockets, as did his wingman. Both missed. The VF-53 section, led by Cdr Robair F. Mohrhardt, had better luck. Their Zunis hit their target, which, gushing smoke, eventually stopped, dead in the water. Stockdale and his wingman joined Mohrhardt, strafing the remaining two communist PTs. The F-8s left one vessel sinking and the other badly damaged.

Two days later a more uncertain engagement "seemed" to have occurred. Radar had alerted the crews aboard *Maddox* and USS *Turner Joy* (DD-951) of another possible North Vietnamese attack, this one on the *Ticonderoga* task group. The two American destroyers opened fire but the contacts vanished from the radar screens. Thirty minutes later, more contacts at 13 miles behind the destroyers suggested another imminent attack. Lookouts on deck and observers at their screens reported possible torpedo wakes in the water. A patrol of A-4s, A-1s and one F-8 from VF-51, overhead the destroyers, were ordered to attack what was believed to be oncoming PT boats. Another section of two A-4s from VA-56 was above an F-8 flown by Cdr Stockdale. Visibility was poor. The pilots could report only ghostly wakes, and bursts of light that might have been gun flashes.

Two hours later, enemy PT boats were again reported. The destroyers, again believing themselves under impending attack, opened fire. Some, including Cdr Stockdale, who was certainly in a good position to see the action, doubted any engagement that night in the Gulf. Indeed, in November 1995, when former Secretary of Defense Robert S. McNamara visited Vietnam, retired Gen Vo Nguyen Giap, the North Vietnamese military leader, was adamant in his denial of a second night's attack. Whatever the reality, President Johnson went on national television to announce retaliatory strikes and increased American presence in South Vietnam.

Cdr Stockdale led the strike – six F-8Es loaded with potent 5-in. diameter Zuni rockets in pods mounted on the characteristic cheek rails below and aft of the cockpits (subsequently, on rare occasions, Zunis were carried along with the F-8's primary missile, the AIM-9D Sidewinder). Stockdale took his flight down, firing Zunis and cannon into a flak site. On the way out, Lt Ray G. "Tim" Hubbard, Stockdale's wingman, strafed an enemy PT boat.

Although the raid was a success, two aircraft and their pilots – both from *Constellation's* CVW-14 – were lost to AAA. The first American Naval Aviator to die in Vietnam, VA-145's Lt(jg) Richard C. Sather, perished when his A-1H Skyraider (BuNo 139760) crashed. Lt(jg) Everett Alvarez of VA-144 ejected from his damaged A-4C Skyhawk (BuNo 149578). He was captured, and subsequently spent eight-and-a-half years as a PoW. A second strike by F-8s from VF-53 on the base at Quang Khe also met with some success.

Although the VPAF already had ten operational bases for its transport, training and radar units by 1963, it lacked fighter bases. Kien An, Gia Lam (Hanoi Airport), Cat Bi and other smaller fields were refurbished from 1955, and the first dedicated fighter base, Noi Bai, was begun with Chinese assistance in 1960 using a 10,000-strong workforce. A large maintenance base was also built at Bach Mai, in Hanoi, to assemble and repair aircraft – Mil Mi-6 helicopters from Gia Lam would transport damaged fighters in as underslung loads. By 1967 Hoa Lac, Tho Xuan and a modern base at Kep were available to defend the heart of the country. Small forward fields were added further south from which B-52s and shipping were attacked.

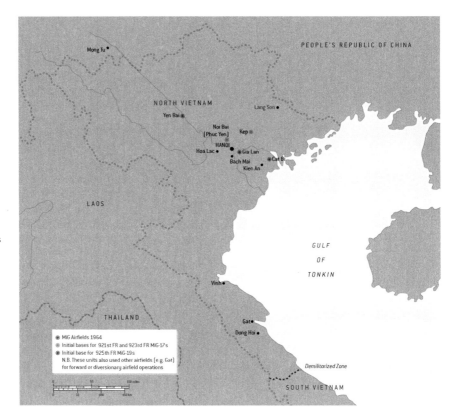

For the next few months ships continued their patrols, but action in Southeast Asia was sporadic. The communists used the lull to move supplies south through Laos. To curtail those activities, the US government initiated two aerial campaigns, namely *Rolling Thunder* (a series of strategic bombing raids against the north's industrial facilities) and *Barrel Roll* (armed reconnaissance missions to monitor the flow of material through Laos), in early 1965. Both operations would involve US Navy and US Marine Corps Crusader squadrons, who would face aerial opposition from the VPAF's small fleet of MiG-17s flown by the 921st FR. Just months earlier, in August 1964, this same unit had flown its MiG-17s from their training base in communist China to the VPAF field at Phuc Yen, north of Hanoi. Although it would be two more years before the first confirmed F-8 kills, there would be engagements between Crusaders and MiG-17s from the spring of 1965.

Two staging areas had been established for US Navy carriers sent into combat, *Dixie Station* to the south and *Yankee Station* in the north. *Dixie* became a warm-up area, with missions flown into South Vietnam in support of Allied ground troops in close contact with the communists – usually Viet Cong guerrillas, who controlled many of the villages. Carrier task groups moved north to *Yankee Station* to fly heavier strikes against North Vietnamese targets in the *Rolling Thunder* campaign. Hanoi and its nearby harbor city Haiphong were the prime recipients of Seventh Fleet Alpha Strikes – flights of A-4s, escorted by F-4s and F-8s that could carry various additional ordnance besides their primary weapon, the Sidewinder and, in the case of the Phantom II, the AIM-7 Sparrow.

Maintenance troops check out a VF-162 Crusader in 1965. The F-8E is armed with four AIM-9Bs. The fuselage pylons that carried Sidewinders and Zunis were unique to the Crusader, giving the jet its characteristic one-two punch unmatched by other naval fighters of the period. (W. F. Flagg)

The location from which the Task Force *77* carrier air wings attacked North Vietnam was known as *Yankee Station*. It was focussed on a point at 16 degrees North and 110 degrees East some 100 miles offshore that had been the start point for the "Yankee Team" armed reconnaissance missions that preceded the war. A *Red Crown* ship 60 miles offshore provided radar coverage of the Red River valley for American strike aircraft, and in July 1966 a Positive Identification and Radar Advisory Zone (PIRAZ) was established with two other vessels to further extend radar coverage and MiG warnings. When on *Yankee Station*, three or four carriers would work in two adjacent operating areas, the northern circle extending 35 nautical miles from a fixed point ZZ. In the northern ("blue") half of this circle, a carrier would alternate its air operations with another flattop in the southern ("gold") semicircle in 12-hour shifts. A second operating circle to the southeast was divided into "red" (north) and "grey" (south) operating areas, working in the same cycle. The southern *Dixie Station* was created on May 15, 1965.

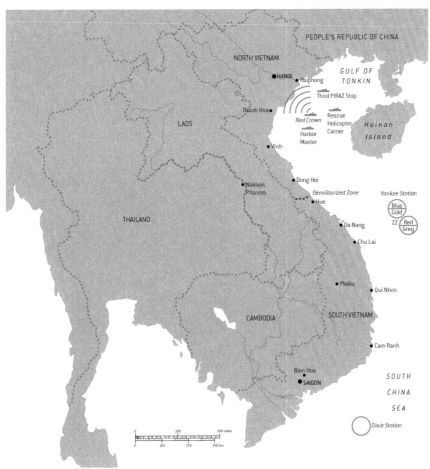

33

Sometimes photos do lie. Pham Ngoc Lan (right) and Tran Hanh examine the gun camera film that appears to show the destruction of a US Navy F-8E from VF-211 on April 3, 1965. However, the badly damaged Crusader made it to Da Nang and was repaired, being returned to flight status. Thus, the MiG pilots' claim to have downed the first aircraft credited to the VPAF was made in error. Nevertheless, the VPAF still lists Lan and Hanh as the first MiG pilots to have shot down an American aircraft. (via Dr István Toperczer)

The MiGs operated under the burden of ground-controlled intercept (GCI), typical of the Soviet doctrine of their pilot training. American fighter crews could choose when and where to confront targets, but the administration in Washington, D.C. levied Rules of Engagement that all too often prohibited outright pursuit and destruction of communist targets, air and ground. Concern for further involving the Soviet Union and particularly communist China, which shared borders with North Vietnam and was openly defensive of its national interests, made for difficult and occasionally dangerous flying – mainly to one's career – for overzealous US crews.

One young VF-162 lieutenant aboard *Oriskany*, Bud Flagg, was on a barrier combat air patrol (BARCAP) mission in 1965. BARCAPs maintained a fighter patrol between the carrier task force and the enemy. Flagg was under the control of a destroyer south of Hong Ghe, the vessel's controller informing him of contacts from the MiG base at Kep. The F-8s were soon vectored to within five miles of the contact, which had turned north. Flagg and his wingman lit their burners and chased after the contact, now headed for the 21st parallel, over which US fighters were not to go. Flagg had the contact on his own small APQ-94 radar scope, which showed that the bogey was now only one or two miles away – almost within range of the F-8's Sidewinders. Flagg only needed five more minutes to close the gap. However, the destroyer controller ordered the Crusader pilots to break off the pursuit, 21st parallel or not, but Flagg and his wingman pressed on. "We all wanted a MiG so bad we could taste it", he remembered. The controller's voice rose to a fever pitch as Flagg crossed the forbidden boundary before finally, reluctantly, turning. He never actually saw the MiG.

The first acknowledged engagement between US Navy F-8s and VPAF MiG-17s occurred on April 3, 1965 during a *Rolling Thunder* strike. The targets were several bridges that formed a key part of vital supply lines to the south. Three A-4s from VA-212 and VA-216 would go after the bridges. Hitting the Dong Phong Thuong Bridge near Ham Rong, VF-211 F-8Es from *Hancock*, armed with Zuni rockets, attacked in sections (two planes each, flown by Lt [later Vice Adm] Jerry Unruh and his wingman, Lt Bobby Hulse, and Lt Cdr Spence Thomas and his wingman, Ens Ray Lorang). Unruh and Hulse followed Thomas and his wingman in a run against flak sites defending the bridge. Clouds and fog obscured the target as Thomas and his wingman climbed back up to 10,000ft.

Six MiG-17s of the 921st FR from Noi Bai, near Hanoi, rose to intercept them. Either by chance or design, the MiGs had mixed with the A-4 formation and stolen in behind the two Crusaders. Two jets homed in on a pair of F-8s whose pilots, now making a second run, were intent on the bridge. MiG driver Pham Ngoc Lan got off a burst. His F-8 prey, flown by Lt Cdr Thomas, seemed to explode. When Lan's gun camera film was developed, it did appear that the American Crusader had indeed been destroyed. Lan received credit for the VPAF's first aerial kill.

The Crusader, BuNo 150845, although severely damaged absorbing Lan's 23mm and 37mm hits in the wings and vertical tail, had, incredibly, remained in the air. Lt Cdr Thomas punched in his afterburner and raced away from the MiGs. His wingman joined up with Lt Unruh's section. Thomas' F-8 had also been hit in the utility hydraulic system, preventing him from raising the fighter's wing for a proper shipboard landing. He diverted to Da Nang, blowing down his landing gear with an emergency air system. The VPAF's first confirmed kill had landed safely ashore. The jet was repaired and returned to flight status, accumulating 4,037 hours before being struck administratively and stored at Davis-Monthan AFB in Tucson, Arizona. Thus, the VPAF claim of the first F-8 kill was wrong.

Pham Ngoc Lan, who was erroneously credited with the Crusader's demise, gave the following detailed account of the engagement:

> My flight consisted of Phan Van Tuc (my wingman), Ho Van Quy and Tran Ming Phuong, while the second flight was made up of Tran Hanh and Pham Giay.
>
> The weather was foggy over Noi Bai air base on April 3, with visibility of between four and five kilometers and 6/10ths cloud, with a base of 300m. Over the anticipated battle area the volume of cloud was 5-6/10ths, with the cloud base up to 700m and visibility of up to ten kilometers. At 0700 hrs the radar operators reported a group of intruding fighters in North Vietnamese airspace, and they left after carrying out their reconnaissance duties. The North Vietnamese command felt that a large formation would subsequently attack the bridge at Ham Rong following this earlier flight. Col Gen Phung The Tai [commander of the VPAF] once again briefed the pilots on their objectives, and ordered a stage-one alert. As anticipated, at 0940 hrs US planes attacked the bridges at Tao, Do Len and Ham Rong.
>
> At 0947 hrs the second flight was launched from Noi Bai. As the leader of the first attack flight, I took off at 0948 hrs and followed a heading of 210 degrees towards the province of Thanh Hoa. Our flight closed to within 45km of the intruders at 1008 hrs, while the second flight was still flying over Ninh Binh Province. I informed air control at 1009 hrs that we had made visual contact with the intruders, and they responded with an order to drop our external fuel tanks and engage the enemy.
>
> The bridge at Ham Rong was attacked in pairs by the American fighter-bombers, which were at this time still unaware of our fighters. My wingman and I quickly latched onto the tails of the two American fighters, and when in range I opened fire with my cannons The F-8 Crusader in front of me exploded in a ball of fire and crashed. I was later credited with the first American fighter-bomber to be shot down by a North Vietnamese fighter pilot.
>
> At the same time the aircraft of Ho Van Quy and Tran Minh Phuong were also pursuing another pair of intruders, with the latter pilot flying as wingman. Ho Van Quy opened fire, but the Americans were out of range and both jets managed to escape. However, the battle between the MiG-17s and the F-8 Crusaders was still far from over in the area of Ham Rong. At 1015 hrs my wingman, Phan Van Tuc, reported on the radio that he had spotted an American fighter to his right, and I immediately replied with an order to attack as I in turn became his wingman. He succeeded in closing in on the American and opened fire with his cannons, eventually causing the F-8 to crash.

Phan Ngoc Lan gets an enthusiastic welcome from his groundcrew after returning from a successful mission – possibly the flight on April 3, 1965. Lan had undertaken his flying training in China, and subsequently became the first VPAF pilot to land at a North Vietnamese airfield in a jet aircraft. Lan used MiG-17F 2050 of the 921st FR to down a USAF CH-53C rescue helicopter on November 6, 1965, sharing the victory with three other pilots from the unit. (via Dr István Toperczer)

At 1017 hrs Phan Van Tuc, Ho Van Quy and Tran Minh Phuong received an order to land, and they duly returned home. In the meantime I was running out of fuel in the vicinity of our airfield, and ground control gave me the order to eject. However, I thought that there was still a chance to save the aircraft, which was of considerable value to the VPAF and still had many more battles left in it! I looked for a suitable landing ground and spotted a long sandy strip on the bank of the Duong River, on which I made a successful landing.

As the air war intensified, strong but friendly competition between F-4 and F-8 crews grew. The two aircraft represented different approaches to fulfilling the same role – protecting the fleet and strike force, and shooting down the opposition. The Naval Aviator flying the F-8 was the direct distillation of decades of US Navy and US Marine Corps fighter pilots. One man in one plane, trained and skilled in tactics, with an overwhelming desire to hunt, find the enemy and destroy him – a quest Crusader squadrons adhered to and practiced daily, ashore or on deployment. The Crusader driver may have had a slight edge on his F-4 counterpart in that the Phantom II, with two engines and a much heavier combat weight, carried no guns, relying instead on two different types of air-to-air missiles. Both weapons (the Sidewinder and the Sparrow) were still in their early stages of maturity, which meant that they suffered development problems that rendered them somewhat undependable. Yet these weapons were all that Phantom II crews had. Each shot was a gamble. The F-8, eventually to gain the sobriquet "last of the gunfighters", had its Colts and, if close enough, the four cannon were devastating.

# THE COMBATANTS

The very rudimentary essentials of fighting a war are thorough knowledge and understanding of the opponent, his capabilities, equipment and his psychology. The price of ignoring this dictum is false confidence and, consequently, gross disadvantage. Nowhere was this more graphically demonstrated than in the early months of the Pacific War in 1941-42. Pearl Harbor notwithstanding, the Imperial Japanese Army and Navy air forces were considered inferior, their pilots being little more than "goggle-eyed midgets" flying aircraft that were shallow copies of western design.

There had been warnings. Claire Chennault, leader of the legendary "Flying Tigers", was painfully aware of the lethal qualities of the Mitsubishi A6M2 Zero-sen. He knew the danger his pilots faced in their seconded Curtiss Tomahawks, yet Chennault's warnings met with indifference from senior officials laboring under the misbelief that the Japanese produced substandard copies of American and European types.

That shortsightedness was repeated with the MiG-17 and its Vietnamese pilots versus the American aviators in the brawny F-4 Phantom II and lithe F-8 Crusader. Although American flight crews were probably less dismissive of the MiG than their fathers had been of the Zero-sen, the prevailing belief was that the Soviet fighter with its inadequately trained pilots would offer no serious trouble. This cavalier attitude encouraged the USAF to curtail its once-active adversary program. The US Navy, too, reduced air combat training. Not until late in the Vietnam War would adversary programs be resuscitated in the form of the US Navy's Topgun Fighter Weapons School at NAS Miramar and the USAF's *Red Flag* exercise at Nellis AFB. *Red Flag* in particular, immeasurably aided by the availability of a number of MiG-17s and MiG-21s (obtained from sources around the world), confirmed that the rugged little MiG-17 was highly maneuverable and a dangerous opponent.

In an objective sense, the MiG's design lacked visibility for the pilot out of its bubble canopy. The fighter's controls, even with hydraulic boost, required considerable force. The MiG was also unstable, possessing "vicious" accelerated stall characteristics – an accelerated stall executed by a pilot new to the aircraft could prove fatal. For all this, and other problems with the diminutive Soviet fighter, it did provide North Vietnamese pilots occasional advantage over their faster, more sophisticated opponents, both F-8 and F-4.

## BACKGROUNDS AND TRAINING

F-8 pilots were direct descendents of the Wildcat and Hellcat aviators of World War II. Flying fast, single-seat, gun-armed fighters, the "jaygees", lieutenants and lieutenant commanders of the Vietnam generation had endured intense, quality flight training, accumulating hundreds of hours of flight time – numbers not obtained by their MiG opponents. American aviators of all services, were (in the majority) college graduates, most from the Naval Academy at Annapolis, the Army at West Point and the newly established Air Force Academy in Colorado Springs. This promoted a study ethic where they could absorb the academic portion of their training syllabi. For those with civilian education, the same study habits trained them in the group culture so essential in a military organization.

Pilots completing the F-8 RAG (Replacement Air Group) syllabus were extremely well trained, more so after Topgun was initiated. F-8 students just completing training and prior to receiving their wings were required to achieve above-average grades of at least 3.1 (out of 4.0). The F-8 student also needed high grades in carrier qualification (understandable, given the difficulty associated with handling a Crusader around the boat). As one veteran F-8 pilot told me, "the Navy was very picky about who went to Crusaders".

The 1966 VF-111 "Sundowners" embarked in *Oriskany*. In the front row, from left to right, are Lt Cdr Pete Peters, unidentified ensign, Lt Lloyd Hyde, Lt Cdr Bob Rasmussen (XO), Cdr Dick Cook (CO), unidentified lieutenant, Lt(jg)s Bob Grammer and Bill McWilliams and Lt Cdr Norm Levey. In the back row, from left to right, are WO Frank Mosoc, Lt Cdr Dick Schaffert, WO Andy Anderson, Lts Ed Van Orden and Randy Rime, Capt Will Abbott (USAF), Lt(jg)s John Sands and Cody Ballasteria, Lt Cdrs Foster S. "Tooter" Teague (who shot down a MiG-17 while flying an F-4 in June 1972) and Bob Pearl and Lt(jg) Jay Meadows. (US Navy)

The last true production model of the F-8 was the "Echo". No new Crusaders were built after the last E-model. Many pilots felt that the Crusader had no equal, being superior to the USAF's F-100 Super Sabre and the US Navy's F4D Skyray, as well as the MiG-17 and more advanced MiG-21. The F-8 was an excellent high-altitude fighter with a 1.8 Mach dash capability and superior high roll rate. With a wing loading at combat weight of 65 pounds per square foot, it also had a very good turn rate – this was at its best when the jet was flying at 325 knots.

On the negative side, the Crusader's cockpit visibility was limited, especially to the rear quarters. But it was dependable and usually available for missions – an attribute most hard-pressed squadron maintenance officers appreciated. Outside of the CO, the billet of maintenance officer is arguably the most difficult in any squadron. Careers can be made or broken by a lack of airplanes to fly.

The F-8's most familiar problems were hydraulic leaks, unsafe or "barber pole" indicators on the leading-edge "droops" (slats on the leading edge of the wings), loss-of-fuel quantity sensors in wing tanks and sensitive wheel brakes, particularly in the heavier F-8E, whose empty weight was 18,800lb, some 2,000lb greater than the earlier models. Along with 9,100lb of JP-5 fuel, an F-8E could carry a variety of bombs and rockets. A frequent load for strike or CAS missions was two huge Mk 84 2,000lb bombs or eight 500lb bombs or eight 5-in. Zuni rockets (one Zuni to a canister, with two canisters on each of four cheek rails for a total of eight) or four AIM-9 Sidewinders. The aircraft also carried 400-500 rounds of 20mm ammunition for the four Colt cannons, two on each side of the fuselage. Compared to an F-4B's 54,800lb, the F-8's maximum catapult weight was 34,000lb.

A late model F-4J's combat weight was 58,000lb. At that combat launch weight the Phantom II could not fight its lighter MiG-17 and MiG-21 opponents. Therefore, before entering an aerial engagement pilots would punch off the underwing fuel tanks and any bombs or other ordnance their aircraft was still carrying. This would reduce their overall weight by several thousand pounds, thus giving the Phantom II a more advantageous weight-to-thrust ratio. The F-4's wing loading was 72lb per square foot (of wing dimensions). The MiG-17's wing loading was 44lb per square foot, making it a more maneuverable fighter.

With a standard air-to-air loadout of two or four Sidewinders, 400-500 rounds of 20mm ammunition and 5,000lb of JP-5 fuel, the F-8E's wing loading was about 65lb per square feet. The E-model's base weight of some 18,800lb rose to 24,000lb when Sidewinders, ammunition and fuel were included – still considerably less than the Phantom II.

Retired US Marine Corps Col Denis J. Kiely remembers:

The F-8 was a beautiful aircraft to fly, both on air-to-air and air-to-ground missions. Good radar, with a 40-mile map mode, 20-nautical-mile detection, 15-nautical-mile lock-on for air targets. But it did have nasty spin characteristics if you let the spin progress. It would not spin inverted, but would flop onto an upright spin if you entered the stall or spin inverted.

The F-8 had great high- and low-altitude performance. It was superior to the F-4 above 20,000ft and a match for it between 15,000ft and 20,000ft. The F-4 was better below 15,000ft.

In contrast to their American counterparts, many North Vietnamese aviators were unschooled country boys, unfamiliar in their youth with airplanes or (beyond a tractor) heavy machinery. They did not have the long tradition of US Naval Academy graduates, nor did they have the civilian student aviation opportunities readily available to young Americans or, for that matter, to Soviet youth. A Vietnamese neophyte pilot very likely had his first flight when he went up with his Russian instructor. The source of VPAF recruits was limited primarily to draft-age young men.

The American military's peacetime new blood came mainly from the military schools, whose graduates, choosing one to two years of flight training, gave the air services their base of regular, career officers. In times of war, however, new pilots and flight crews were needed beyond what the academies could provide. For this, the services relied on civilian colleges' Reserve Officer Training Corps (ROTC) and the US Navy's Officer Candidate School (OCS), located at Newport, Rhode Island. OCS was mainly for the ship side, the "black shoes", as opposed to the aviation "brown shoes". OCS graduates could apply for flight training, however.

In 1955, another venue for US Navy officer flight crewmen had been created with the establishment of the Aviation Officer Candidate School (AOCS) in Pensacola, Florida. Originally a 15-week course, by 1968 AOCS was reduced to 11 weeks to accommodate the demand for more pilots and Naval Flight Officers (NFOs) created

# ENGAGING THE ENEMY

As an engagement progressed, and an F-8 pilot could hopefully maneuver himself somewhere in his quarry's rear quarter, his AIM-9 would start its characteristic "growl", letting him know its infrared seeker was "sniffing" and eventually acquiring its target, gradually getting louder in his headphones. As the Naval Aviator closed the gap between himself and the MiG, and if the MiG pilot went into afterburner to escape, the Sidewinder's seeker head would conclusively acquire the enemy fighter. The indications on the gunsight would confirm this, at which point the F-8 pilot would press the button on the control column to fire the AIM-9. If there was no growl, he recycled the switch to select another missile, which, once launched, would find its way to the target.

The earlier AIM-9B had a primitive un-cooled seeker head, while the AIM-9D's head was cooled by compressed nitrogen stored in a bottle contained in the launcher rack. The compressed gas expanded through a small orifice in the seeker head, creating very low temperatures that improved the seeker's discrimination. The small armament panel was located below the main panel in the cockpit. Mounted on the panel was a toggle switch that controlled the missile head coolant, which lasted about 2.5 hours. Another toggle was the "master arm" switch which, when off, rendered the

rotary armament selector "dead". Other toggles controlled the 20mm cannon, while the rotary switch permitted selection of different Sidewinders as well as any underwing ordnance.

The F-8 was of course "the last of the gunfighters", and if the Sidewinders did not do their job, the Crusader pilot could hopefully resort to his four 20mm cannon – and many did, with widely varying degrees of success. A few MiG killers did use a combination of missiles and guns to finally score their victories. Amongst the few F-8 pilots credited with a guns kill was Lt Cdr Robert Kirkwood, who commented, "One of the ironies of the F-8's story was that it was called 'the last of the gunfighters', but it was equipped with an unreliable, inaccurate, ineffective gun system".

The control column's grip had two red buttons that "pickled" bombs as well as a trigger on the front face that fired the cannon. Although the various F-8 models changed the control column's "layout", the sequence of activating and firing a Sidewinder remained constant – Master Arm – on, select the missile station for firing and depress the "pickle" switch on the control column, holding it down until the missile left the rail (one- to two-second delay).

Early on, the trigger switch fired the missile and all other ordnance. However, when it became advantageous to

have both the missiles and the cannon "hot" during an engagement, the top button was rewired to release missiles (or bombs), while the trigger remained the way to fire the guns. Before all this, the top button was used to activate or deactivate the autopilot. Later, another panel was added below the canopy rail that allowed the pilot to select either the top two guns or the bottom two, thus extending the precious seconds of 20mm firing duration.

Typically, pilots would turn on the Sidewinder cooling, then the Master Arm switch, select either bombs or missiles (depending on the mission) using the rotary switch and arm the guns while still feet wet approaching North Vietnam. Of course, on a BARCAP, where the F-8s remained over the water, pilots would arm the guns and missiles shortly after launch. If his Crusader was not carrying bombs, the pilot would set up the guns charged and ready and have one of the fuselage positions (missile launchers)

selected. With the Master Arm switch on, this meant that pressing the pickle switch would fire a Sidewinder and pulling the trigger would fire the guns.

As far as the radar was concerned, it may have given crude ranging information but this was really of academic interest. Perhaps the pilot would give it a quick glance during a mission, but nothing more. It took the pilot's full attention to operate the radar properly, and during a real engagement he was more occupied looking *outside* the cockpit. None of the F-8 kills had anything to do with the Crusader's radar.

Typical of flightline discussion groups in communist countries, VPAF pilots and their groundcrews go over the last mission in the shade provided by the tail of a "Fresco-A" at Noi Bai in 1965. This version of the MiG-17 lacked afterburner. Other canvas-covered "Fresco-As" can be seen parked in the distance. (via Dr István Toperczer)

by the conflict in Vietnam. Indeed, AOCS pumped out weekly classes of 40 to 60 new ensigns during the Vietnam War, all scheduled for pilot training at Pensacola's NAS Saufley Field or NFO training with VT-10 at NAS Sherman Field, at the other end of the Pensacola Main Site complex. When AOCS finally closed its doors in September 2007, 55,000 men and, later, women had graduated from the course.

Pilot training normally lasted some 18 months, while NFO training, depending on the aircraft to be flown, ran for about a year. The longest NFO syllabus was 18 months for Naval Aviators destined to crew the E-2 Hawkeye. The shortest was the jet navigator course for A-3s, which ran for just four-to-six weeks at NAS Glynco, Georgia. Training for the F-4 RIO and A-6 BN (bombardier-navigator) was almost a year, with four months at Pensacola following commissioning and preflight and another three or four months at Glynco. Although he would have received his wings at Glynco, the new NFO then went to his advanced training squadron to convert to the specific aircraft he would fly in the fleet. For BNs, it was VA-42 at NAS Oceana in Virginia Beach, Virginia. New RIOs went to VF-101 at Oceana or VF-121 at NAS Miramar, California, north of San Diego, or VMFAT-101 for the US Marine Corps at MCAS El Toro, near Los Angeles.

For those new aviators assigned to fly the F-8, post-graduate training was at VF-124 at Miramar and VF-174 at NAS Cecil Field, Jacksonville, Florida. Eventually, all Crusader training was assumed by VF-124, VF-174 becoming VA-174 as the RAG for the A-7 Corsair II light attack aircraft that would replace the A-4.

Training of new jet pilots was all very involved, and seemingly endless. Students finished primary training, then primary *jet* training at NAS Meridian, Mississippi, and introductory training flying from carriers, culminating in a trip to a vessel (usually the World War II veteran USS *Lexington* (CVT-16), now a training carrier) for their first "traps", or arrested landings. By the time a pilot, now endowed with the romantic title "Naval Aviator", joined his fleet squadron he might have close to 400 hours. Not a huge number, but enough for sufficient experience and understanding of his trade, and the forces he could use whenever he took off, or "launched" (the US Navy jargon for leaving the runway or flightdeck). When returning, he "recovered" or "trapped", these terms usually being reserved for a successful arrested landing aboard the carrier. The word "landing" is too soft, too quiet, and improperly conveys a Naval Aviator having brought himself and his aircraft to a successful flight conclusion.

Academic success or capability bore little on a Vietnamese recruit's fighter pilot potential. Before acceptance into flight training, the recruit had to demonstrate patriotism, be fit and healthy and possess a "killer instinct". He would disdain the pilot-shooter/wingman tactic of American aviators. The team concept, hunting together, was better suited to communist thinking. Total enemy aircraft destroyed, not individual scores, was the desired end.

When the first MiG-17-qualified VPAF pilots arrived at Noi Bai airfield on August 6, 1964 they had been training on the "Fresco" for up to four years. Indeed, the initial cadre of trainees had been in China and Russia since March 1956. Some 50 aspiring fighter pilots in China, commanded by Pham Dung, were supported in North Vietnam by the First Flying School at Cat Bi and the Second Flying School at Gia

Dao Dinh Luyen was a senior aviator in the VPAF, having been the first fighter wing commander as well as the leader of the first group of trainees in China. In February 1964 he became the leader of the 921st FR, and that August brought the first group of MiG-17s to North Vietnam from China. In 1977 he became the head of the VPAF. Luyen does not appear to have been credited with any kills during the war, despite the MiG-17F in this photograph being marked with three victory stars. (via Dr István Toperczer)

Lam from 1956 onwards. Others were trained in Czechoslovakia as Ho Chi Minh's dream of an air force took shape. His recruits made up in enthusiasm for their deficiencies in basic technical education or physical fitness. All had to be taught basic Russian to understand the aircraft manuals and their instructors. Their political motivation was invariably strong but it was constantly tested by their mentors, who regarded unswerving devotion to their patriotic cause as equal in importance to aptitude as a pilot. Often, more than three-quarters of students failed to complete the flight-training courses and were relegated to ground duties.

A shortage of aircraft and the lack of a suitable airfield in North Vietnam meant that the first group of pilots remained in China after "graduating" on the MiG-17, flying MiG-15s instead. Generally, the Vietnamese students felt more "at home" with Chinese tutors and had fewer communications problems than those being trained in Russia, despite the presence of translators. MiG-17s were soon provided for them at Son Dong, where the VPAF's first groundcrew were being instructed. In 1963 the entire operation was moved to Mong Tu, close to the North Vietnamese border. This base shift coincided with the arrival of 36 Soviet-supplied MiG-17Fs.

1. Rudder neutral trim light
2. Aileron neutral trim light
3. Speed brake light
4. In-flight refueling probe light
5. Wings-wheel-droop warning light
6. Landing gear position indicators (three)
7. Engine pressure ratio indicator
8. Tachometer
9. Angle-of-attack indicator
10. Inflight refueling probe switch
11. Engine oil pressure indicator
12. Radio altitude indicator
13. Fire warning light
14. Fire warning test switch
15. Fire control radar scope
16. Gunsight
17. Fuel low-level warning light
18. Engine fuel pump warning light
19. Course indicator (ILS indicator)
20. Navigation (bearing-distance-heading) indicator (gyro compass)
21. Fuel dump switch
22. Fuel transfer switch
23. Fuel transfer pump caution light
24. Clock
25. UHF present channel indicator
26. Oxygen warning light
27. Transfer fuel quantity indicator
28. Hydraulic pressure indicators
29. Engine oil and hydraulic pressure warning light
30. Liquid oxygen quantity indicator
31. Main fuel quantity indicator
32. Fuel flow indicator
33. Fuel quantity test switch
34. Turn-and-bank indicator
34A. Fuel boost pumps warning light
35. Attitude indicator
36. Nose trim indicator
37. Armament panel
38. Altimeter
39. Airspeed-Mach number indicator
40. Acceleration indicator
41. Rate-of-climb indicator
42. Exhaust temperature indicator
43. Cockpit lighting
44. Angle-of-attack indexer
45. Wet compass
46. Wing downlock handle
47. Wing incidence handle
48. Wing incidence release switch
49. Throttle
50. Emergency brake handle
51. Left-hand switch panel
52. Engine master switch
53. Yaw stabilization switch
54. Emergency pitch trim handle
55. Yaw stabilization light
56. Roll stabilization light
57. Autopilot master switch
58. Autopilot heading hold disable switch
59. Emergency power handle
60. Autopilot engaged light
61. Landing gear handle
62. Emergency pitch trim channel
63. Roll stabilization switch
64. Throttle catapult handle
65. Throttle friction wheel
66. Radar set control panel
67. Fire control panel
68. Arresting gear handle
69. Engine and icing indicator lights
70. Engine anti-icing switch
71. Pitot heat switch
72. Cockpit pressure altimeter
73. Emergency power indicator light
74. Emergency generator switch
75. Air-conditioning panel
76. Autopilot control panel
77. TACAN panel
78. Exterior lights control panel
79. Interior lights control panel
80. Armament panel dimming knob
81. Cockpit emergency air ventilation knob
82. Interior lights dimming panel
83. Compass panel
84. UHF panel
85. Master generator switch
86. Main generator indicator
87. Control column
88. Control grip with roll trim knob, pitot trim knob, trigger switch, autopilot engaged/disengage switch and nose gear steering switch
89. Radar antenna control stick
90. Rudder pedals
91. Martin-Baker Aircraft Mk 5 ejection seat
92. Emergency harness release handle

Three years earlier, on May 1, 1960, construction of the modern Noi Bai airfield had begun, and the base was ready for the VPAF's single squadron, the 921st FR, when it was led in by Dao Dinh Luyen on August 6, 1964.

Before venturing into combat, 921st FR pilots continued intensive training with increased flying hours in their MiG-17 "silver swallows" and MiG-15UTI trainers, supported by long sessions in primitive simulator cockpits. Aware that their fighters were inferior in numbers and technology to the Americans' equipment, VPAF personnel worked with their Soviet and Chinese advisors for another four months on tactics to integrate the obsolescent MiG-17 into North Vietnam's rapidly-developing network of AAA sites and radar. Like American pilots, they studied the tactics of World War II aces and worked on the assumption that "whoever fires first wins".

Selection of suitable pilots for the first combat-ready sections of the squadron was a rigorous process. Some of the more over-enthusiastic individuals, including a few who favored "kamikaze" ramming tactics, were restrained within the rigid doctrines of GCI taught by Soviet instructors. Some Vietnamese controllers,

**F-8E CRUSADER COCKPIT**

Col Nguyen Van Bay, the VPAF's ranking MiG-17 ace with seven victories, conducts a class in air combat tactics for a trio of new pilots. He is sitting on the wreckage of an unidentified US aircraft. Bay claimed three Crusaders destroyed, two of which tallied with US Navy losses. (via Dr István Toperczer)

including Le Thanh Chon, were former MiG-17 pilots. In action, pilots became accustomed to sleeping under their MiGs while on alert duty and "scrambling" before 0800 hrs.

When American air attacks began in earnest in 1965, the VPAF studied the predictable routes that the restrictive rules of engagement forced the US Navy and USAF to follow to their targets. Interception tracks were duly planned to minimize exposure to enemy fighters and to take advantage of proximity to home territory and defenses. Essentially, the pilots soon realized that they would have to orbit as "point defense" fighters close to likely targets, climbing from low altitude to hit the intruders. New bases were planned to place the short-range MiGs close to strategic targets. Above all, the country's radar network was extended to give sufficient warning of attack, particularly from the seaward side.

Flying was often limited by the Vietnamese climate, but this had been the same in the USSR, where the weather confined flying training to the summer. In Russia, dogfighting training had been quite limited, and the VPAF pilots' small stature and light weight (sometimes below the minimum for safe use of the ejection seat) became a real handicap as they wrestled with the heavy controls of the MiG-17.

Basic training was initially performed on the piston-engined Yak-18 and, after 1966, on Czech-built L-29 Delfin jets, with 80 hours on this type followed by 40 hours on the MiG-17 at Kushchovsaya air base. A few L-29s were passed to the VPAF in 1971.

The MiG-17 was considered obsolescent in Russia by mid-1957, being used only for ground attack (for which it was not really suited) or training. The perceived wisdom on the MiG-17 versus other jet fighters was limited to the assessment of Chinese J-5s in evenly matched combat with Taiwanese F-86Fs in 1960, or Egyptian and Syrian examples fighting Israeli Mystere IVAs in 1956 and 1960. Nothing was known about the aircraft's chances against more advanced American types. VPAF pilots had to establish those rules for themselves. Pham Ngoc Lan, senior pilot in the 921st FR in the spring of 1965, is credited with working out attack patterns that gave his squadron its first success against US Navy F-8s in April of that year. His training in China had lasted six years.

Another 30 pilots returned during the summer of 1965 from courses at Krasnodar Flight Officers' School on the Black Sea coast, where aviators from all corners of the communist bloc were trained at a four-airfield complex. These men formed the nucleus of the second MiG-17 unit, the 923rd "Yen The" Fighter Regiment. At the same time the 921st FR began to induct its first MiG-21 pilots. Flying the MiG-21 was the ambition of most MiG-17 pilots, but there were few examples available until later in the war.

Following the arrival of 18 more Krasnodar-trained pilots in November 1966, the VPAF's own 910th "Julius Fucik" Training Regiment began to produce aircrew. The first 14 were ready for action in January 1968, and all would be needed. By war's end North Vietnamese records listed 168 pilots killed in action – a large number for such a small country.

Pilot numbers (34) early in 1964 were less than the numbers of available aircraft, but the training program managed to generate more than three pilots for each MiG by 1970, despite a persistent lack of trainer aircraft.

Each fighter regiment had two or three squadrons on strength, each with at least eight fighters, commanded by a captain or lieutenant. Squadrons were in turn divided into flights, and pilots learned to operate as two pairs, or as a three-aircraft interception flight with a "lone wolf" killer MiG-17 some distance behind the leading pair.

VPAF pilots engaging the F-8 in the early stages of the Vietnam conflict would discover that the aircraft was appreciably faster than their MiG-17s and competitively maneuverable. The Crusader's 20mm cannon packed a genuine punch, but so did the MiG-17's three heavy guns. Psychologically, the men in the cockpits were at opposite ends of the spectrum. The US Navy F-8 pilot was better trained, with more flight hours, and thoroughly indoctrinated into the ethic of the fighter pilot and the squadron. He was also espousing the dictates of his own nation – and his own sworn duties – and was therefore committed to an independent and democratically free South Vietnam. His North Vietnamese opponent, albeit less trained and with relatively less sophisticated equipment, was fighting over, and for, his country. For him, the Allied effort was an unwanted intervention into a civil war of the Vietnamese people, and in his view a brutal invasion of his homeland.

# MIG-17F "FRESCO-C" COCKPIT

1. ASP-4NM gunsight
2. Throttle
3. Push-to-talk radio control
4. Aileron trim control
5. Flap and airbrake levers
6. ARK-5 radio compass tuning panel
7. Emergency canopy jettison
8. Cartridge-fired ejection seat
9. Ejection handles (both sides of seat)
10. Rudder pedals
11. Extendable control column with gun, speedbrake and ordnance/tank jettison buttons
12. Ordnance control panel
13. Emergency landing gear control
14. Canopy lock (right)
15. Canopy lock (left)
16. Windscreen de-mist and ventilation
17. Main pneumatic air pressure gauge
18. Main hydraulic pressure gauge
19. Aileron trim switches
20. Map/document holder

21. Bullet-proof windshield (64mm/2.5in. thick)
22. Side-light transparency (8mm/0.31in. thick)
23. Canopy sealing hose, pressurised to 3 bars (42.8psi)
24. KUS-1200 airspeed indicator
25. VD-17 altimeter
26. RV-2 radio altimeter
27. AGI-1 artificial horizon
28. EUP-46 turn-and-bank indicator (electric)
29. MS-15 Mach meter
30. VAR-75 vertical speed indicator
31. Padded gunsight reticle adjusting knob
32. White stripe for positioning control column in spin recovery
33. Pneumatic brakes control "bicycle" lever
34. Electrical panel
35. Panels for fire detection, fuel control and engine ignition
36. KES 857 fuel gauge

37. Landing gear select indicator
38. Flare select switch
39. Brake pressure gauge
40. ARK-5 Automatic Direction-Finding (ADF) indicator
41. DGMK-3 gyro compass display
42. EMI-3P fuel and oil pressure/temperature indicators
43. TE-15 engine rpm indicator
44. TGZ-47 engine exhaust gas temperature gauge
45. EM-10M indicator
46. Gyro-compass "align to north" button
47. Pilot's oxygen indicator
48. Undercarriage control handle
49. Undercarriage position indicator
50. Flap switch
51. VA-340 volt/ampere indicator
52. Master electrical switch
53. Cockpit over-pressure indicator
54. Extra armament control panel (some aircraft)

# COMBAT

On April 9, 1965, F-4Bs from VF-96, embarked in *Ranger*, apparently strayed over communist Chinese-controlled Hainan Island and were engaged by People's Liberation Navy Air Force Shenyang J-5s (license-built MiG-17Fs). One Phantom II shot down a communist fighter, only to be downed itself minutes later. The F-4B crew, Lt(jg) Terry Murphy and his RIO, Ens Ron Fegan, were presumed to have been killed in action – both men were eventually awarded a confirmed kill. In the next few months the air war began heating up, resulting in the VPAF losing five MiG-17s and the USAF two F-4s. All this action had involved F-4 Phantom IIs, not F-8 Crusaders, but that would soon change.

The US was sending massive numbers of Army and Marine Corps ground troops into South Vietnam. The North Vietnamese, nurturing a growing fleet of advanced MiG-21s, were building an air force. The USAF and the US Marine Corps were constructing impressive air bases in South Vietnam. And, in ever-increasing strength, the US Navy was deploying its fleet of aircraft carriers. There were five main categories of carriers – the "27C class", or "27-Charlies", World War II *Essex* class ships that in their day had been the world's largest flattops; the *Midway* class vessels *Midway*, *Franklin D. Roosevelt* and *Coral Sea*; the *Forrestal* class, USS *Forrestal* (CVA-59), USS *Saratoga* (CVA-60), *Ranger* and USS *Independence* (CVA-62); the three *Kitty Hawk* class ships, *Kitty Hawk*, *Constellation* and USS *America* (CVA-66); and, finally, the only ship of its class, the nuclear-powered USS *Enterprise* (CVAN-65).

In the initial stages of the conflict the F-8 fighter (VF) squadrons provided escort and CAS for ground operations. The light photo (VFP) RF-8 was a dedicated reconnaissance platform and carried no weapons. The F-8C/D, depending on its mission, could only carry Zuni rockets and Sidewinders. A variety of weapons could be affixed to the "Echo's" underwing pylons, including the Mk 84 2,000lb bomb –

often a game changer for ground troops in close enemy contact. The Zunis were particularly effective against individual, specific targets such as small boats and supply trains.

Thanks to flak and newly introduced surface-to-air missiles (SAMs), F-8 losses mounted as Operation *Rolling Thunder* got into its stride. By June 1966 aerial activity on both sides had dramatically increased, and that month the Crusader finally achieved its first victory after a handful of close encounters during 1965. The VPAF had enlarged its fighter force to the point where two squadrons were equipped with MiG-17s, one of which was now also converting to the MiG-21. The first encounters were actually tests, with each side endeavoring to discover, in man and in machine, the opponent's weak point. Of F-8 versus MiG-17, the technologies were not so much in question as were the individual aviators. Each side had much to learn. For American aviators, the MiG-17, when flown by a skilled and aggressive pilot, could offer a surprising defense.

## FIRST KILLS

June 12, 1966 saw *Hancock* launch an A-4 strike composed of Skyhawks from VA-212 and VA-216, escorted by Crusaders from VF-211 and VF-24. From 1,500ft below the clouds VF-211's CO, Cdr Harold Marr, and his wingman Lt(jg) Phil Vampatella and the two-plane VF-24 section led by Lt Cdr Fred Richardson (one of the US Navy's few black aviators at the time) monitored the A-4s coming off their attack runs. Vampatella spotted four MiG-17s racing in behind the Skyhawk formation at the "seven o'clock" position and slightly above at 2,000ft.

Marr led his section into a hard turn to meet them. Two MiGs split off, leaving Marr and Vampatella to face the other two head on. One was all silver, the other gray, both with red stars on the wing uppersurfaces and rear fuselage. Both were clean externally, with no tanks or missiles. Marr fired a short burst from his cannons "more for courage than anything else", he said later, "just to hear my four cannons bang". The F-8s were doing about 450 knots and pulling 7-8G in a reverse hard right in a sharp scissors. "I got a good 90-degree deflection gun shot, but my cannon missed again, and Phil went after one and I went after the other".

Marr was now at 2,500ft, above and behind the MiG, which was low, at 1,500ft, running out of altitude. Marr fired the first of his two AIM-9D IR-seeker Sidewinders, but the missile simply fell away and hit the ground. "The MiG had been in 'burner for four or five minutes", Marr recalled, "so it had to be low on fuel. The pilot rolled away and headed for his base. I rolled in behind, stuffed it in 'burner and closed at 500 knots. At a half mile I fired my last 'Winder, and it chopped off his tail and starboard wing. The poor pilot didn't have a chance to eject".

Lt Cdr Richardson, meanwhile, had targeted the second MiG of the two that had split off, shooting both his missiles unsuccessfully. His wingman, Lt(jg) Denis C. Duffy Jr, had fired a Sidewinder that also failed to reach the MiG.

Cdr Hal Marr returns from his historic MiG-killing mission of June 12, 1966. His plane captain attends to safing the Crusader's ejection seat on the deck of *Hancock* before the pilot exits his aircraft. (US Navy)

Marr, who had destroyed the formation leader, now saw two more MiGs, one gray, the other in the green-brown camouflage that would occasionally be seen during the war (aircraft in this scheme were appropriately labeled "snakes" by the VPAF pilots themselves) orbiting above him at "nine o'clock". Marr climbed to 6,000ft to take on the second pair, firing a short cannon burst (perhaps no more than 25 rounds) that shattered the right wing of one of the jets. Then, seemingly out of ammunition, he was forced to disengage. In reality, Marr's two lower cannon had not fired because of an electrical problem. Cdr Marr's official score for June 12, 1966 remains one MiG confirmed and one probable.

These dark green MiG-17Fs of the 923rd FR were photographed on the ramp at Kep in 1968. VPAF pilots nicknamed these camouflaged aircraft "Snakes" because of their color schemes. 2077 had arrived at Kep in late 1965 as part of the second batch of "Fresco-Cs" delivered to the VPAF. In the early days at Kep there were no shelters for the 923rd FR to keep their aircraft in, so they were painted green overall and hidden under trees. (via Dr István Toperczer)

On his return to *Hancock* he made the traditional victory fly-by, and in all his excitement Marr forgot to drop his tailhook and had to make a second approach – such a mistake usually resulted in the perpetrator having to pay a $5 fine. *Hancock's* CO, Capt Jim Donaldson, sportingly radioed Marr that he, himself, would pay the fine.

The "legend" of Hal Marr's second MiG has had a long life. Someone, *somewhere* has authorized the confirmation of Marr's second kill. Either the MiG crashed or its pilot may have ejected. Even the VPAF has confirmed the loss of the second MiG-17. Marr passed away in 2001 without learning of the change to his second kill's status.

This second meeting of the F-8 and MiG-17 provides some insight into the two different types, and their pilots. It was still early in the war, and intelligence on either side regarding their opponent was sparse. Cdr Marr had used the turning ability of his F-8 to great advantage, and the Crusader's faster speed enabled him to reach the departing MiGs in time to hit the second one. Clearly, in that first encounter, despite their heavier armament, the MiGs and their pilots seemed no match for the Americans. This would change.

## NEXT ENCOUNTERS

On June 21, two Crusader flights launched from *Hancock* on different missions. A solitary F-8E from VF-211 was tasked with escorting an RF-8A from VFP-63 Det L, while three more "Checkmates'" Crusaders covered six A-4s. The photo-reconnaissance RF-8 would take post-strike bomb damage assessment (BDA) photos. The three escorts were flown by Lt Cdr Cole Black, Lt Gene Chancy and Lt(jg) Vampatella.

The strike started badly, with the RF-8A flown by Lt Leonard C. Eastman being shot down (his loss being credited by the VPAF to Phan Van Tuc, Phan Thanh Trung, Duong Truong Tan, and Nguyen Van Bay). After first determining that the A-4s were safely away following their attack runs, the escort pilots found Eastman's crash site. Black and Chancy orbited overhead while Vampatella joined up with the photo escort, Lt Dick

# PHILIP VICTOR VAMPATELLA

Born on March 31, 1940 in the family home in Islip, Long Island, New York, Phil Vampatella was one of six children, whose mother and father had emigrated from Italy in 1912. Phil was the youngest of two boys and four girls. His father, Philip, a carpenter, had served in World War I, then bought land and built a house. The family was close-knit and happy. During World War II his father had worked at Grumman, while Philip's older brother, Biagio, or Ben, enlisted in the US Navy. Phil was a newspaper boy, popular in school. He had developed an early interest in flying, and he and his father would often drive to MacArthur Airfield to watch the planes – a familiar start for a young boy who wanted to fly. Phil was athletic and played Little League baseball and shot hoops with his friends after school, using a basketball hoop in the backyard.

A good student, he did well in high school, both academically and in sports. Math and science were his best subjects, and he was elected to the National Honor Society, a great honor for a young high school student. Although it would be a struggle for the family, there was no doubt that the youngest child would go to college. Phil had been accepted by two fine colleges, Syracuse University and Rutgers, the State University of New Jersey. He chose Rutgers, a good engineering school, which is what he wanted to study. However, even with his success in high school, Phil had trouble combining college courses with a busy schedule of participating in too many clubs. His mother's death in 1958 during his sophomore year devastated Phil, and he began to study less and fail more at school. Finally, the university had to let him go.

After working in construction jobs he started thinking about the military. A recruiter told the young man about opportunities in the US Navy's Aviation Cadet Program. With two years of college, he could earn the Gold Wings of a Naval Aviator as well as an ensign's Naval Reserve commission. Then he could progress through courses to a college degree. It was too good a deal to ignore, and Phil signed up. He found himself part of a young group of 50 men at Pensacola's Aviation Cadet

Indoctrination course. They were the daily recipients of the attention of Marine Corps drill instructors – sergeants, staff sergeants and gunnery sergeants, all highly selected experienced enlisted Marines dedicated to preparing young civilians to enter a new life as leaders and as Naval Aviators. This organization eventually became the US Navy's well-known Aviation Officer Candidate School, portrayed, with varying degrees of accuracy, in the popular 1982 film *An Officer and a Gentleman*.

The physical training was intense, followed by courses in US Navy subjects such as Naval Justice and Leadership. Everything in the course was focused on attention to detail, a mundane topic that many people, especially young men, overlook. But in the business of flying, particularly flying fast military aircraft, and most importantly, flying from an aircraft carrier, it is the basis of survival and success in the mission. Phil experienced few problems. He was selected for jet training and eventually got his wings and commission in February 1964. He was also assigned to VF-124, the training squadron for future F-8 pilots. He then went to VF-211. His first choice was the A-4 Skyhawk, then the F-4 Phantom II, then the F-8.

At first the Crusader proved to be the handful Phil had heard about. But each flight increased his confidence in handling the Vought thoroughbred. Finally arriving at VF-211, Phil deployed with his new squadron to the Pacific, and then to Southeast Asia, where he made his first combat flights over North Vietnam in 1965. His second cruise was just as eventful because it was on that deployment that he scored his MiG-17 kill and received the first Navy Cross awarded to a fighter pilot in Vietnam.

Returning from his 1966 deployment, Phil left active duty but remained in the reserves. He was going to fly A-4s with a squadron at Floyd Bennett Field, just outside New York City, but just before he officially signed on the squadron was recalled to active duty during the 1968 Pueblo Crisis. He was not ready to go back to the Fleet and possible combat duty, so he left the reserves. Phil later flew as an airline pilot for Pan Am and United and eventually retired to Maine, where he lives today, occasionally enjoying reunions with other Crusader alumni.

Lt(jg) Phil Vampatella

# PHAM NGOC LAN

While not an ace — he is officially credited with three kills — Pham Ngoc Lan had his first few minutes of fame, or historical importance, because he is considered to be, at least in Vietnam, the first VPAF pilot to have shot down an American fighter. Unfortunately, that claim is not correct. One of four MiG-17 pilots who fought VF-211 F-8s on April 3, 1965, Pham was born on December 12, 1934, in the Diem Nam Dong ward, Dien Ban district, Quang Nam province of North Vietnam, then Indochina. At the age of ten, with World War II raging, he joined a Young Patriot Team to collect food for his country's defense force. His father encouraged his patriotic spirit, having convinced a friend who was the Police commander of Dak Lak province (Phu Yen City) to let his son join the team. Pham was quick and smart, a good swimmer and good in rowing and horse riding. He also spoke French very well, having learned the language in school.

In 1952, aged 18, Pham enlisted in the 84th Regiment and was assigned to the 30th Sapper Battalion. In October 1954 he was sent to high school, the only soldier to be so selected from his entire division. After finishing high school, he was offered the chance to choose what he wanted to do in the army. Pham remembered a film that featured tank action during the final assault on Berlin in May 1945, so he wrote that down on the form, hoping one day to participate in an assault on Saigon's presidential palace. However, the VPAF needed pilots, and he was ordered to flight training. One of the other young men he trained with was Nguyen Ngoc Do, a future MiG-21 ace with six kills. The group studied in communist China until August 6, 1964 when they returned home to fly MiG-17s against US Navy and USAF air strikes.

On April 3, 1965 at 0946 hrs, Pham was the flight leader for four MiG-17s from the 921st FR that took off to intercept an American strike group approaching the Ham Rong Bridge. The account of the first engagement between F-8s and MiG-17s has been given in the main text. Pham received credit at the time for shooting down the first American aircraft to fall to a VPAF pilot. The date was later honored as VPAF Day. Returning from the fight, Pham found that his compass had been damaged and he had to navigate by eye, following the Ba Lat River to the Red River, flying at an altitude of only 600ft. Realizing that he would not be able to reach his base at Noi Bai before running out of fuel, Pham crash-landed on a river bank. His MiG, No. 2310, was later recovered and went on to fly again before being transferred to a flying school.

Pham flew throughout the war, gaining a shared kill credit for a USAF CH-3C helicopter on November 6, 1965. He later transitioned to the MiG-21 and, as a captain, served as vice commander of the 921st FR. In this capacity Pham regularly led VPAF fighters into action against American strike formations. In April 1975 he helped train former MiG-17 pilots in transitioning to the American A-37B Dragonfly light attack aircraft (an armed version of the Cessna T-37 "Tweet" USAF trainer) that were left by the retreating South Vietnamese air force.

Pham served in various assignments in the post-war VPAF, rising in rank to major general and retiring in August 1999. He was honored with a designation of People's Armed Forces Hero in 2010. Pham presently lives in Hanoi and pursues a variety of interests including music.

Phan Ngoc Lan

Lt(jg) Vampatella relives his MiG-killing mission of June 21, 1966 in true fighter pilot fashion in VF-211's ready room on board *Hancock*. (US Navy)

Smith, who had assumed the traditional role of on-scene search and rescue (SAR) commander. The four F-8s were at 1,500ft to 2,000ft above the crash site when the A-4s called out SAM launches and MiG warnings. Sure enough, the F-8s began drawing flak, with Vampatella's jet being hit. It suffered some tail section damage, but not enough to keep him out of action, and despite running low on fuel he remained on station for ten to twelve minutes until Black ordered him and Smith to find a tanker.

Eastman's parachute could be seen on the ground, so Black and Chancy climbed to 6,000ft for better radio reception with the incoming SAR helicopter. After making contact with the latter, they went down to 2,000ft directly above Eastman's crashed RF-8, where Chancy spotted an orange signal flare a half-a-mile away, and at the same time Black saw two MiG-17s sliding in from the south out of the clouds at the F-8s' "two o'clock". The VPAF fighters were within half-a-mile of the Crusaders, the VF-211 jets being 500ft below the MiGs. Black fired his cannon as the enemy fighters – also firing their guns – passed close to Chancy, who fired his own guns as he crossed from left to right over Black. The MiGs had obviously waited for the Americans to leave their high-altitude station and start orbiting above the RF-8 crash site.

Chancy's fire hit the MiG wingman, blowing a wing off the fighter. "He was so close", the F-8 pilot later recalled, "I could have counted his teeth". Although Gene Chancy is certain his initial gunfire downed the MiG (flown by Duong Truong Tan of the 923rd FR, who ejected), and therefore considers himself one of the few F-8 drivers to claim a Vietnam gun kill, he had also fired a Sidewinder, which was officially

The extent of the flak damage inflicted on Vampatella's Crusader on June 21, 1966 is evident. Shortly after being hit by AAA Vamptella downed his MiG, thus proving the F-8's ruggedness. (US Navy)

listed as the means by which he achieved his June 21, 1966 kill. However, a recent listing of US Navy aerial victories in Vietnam has changed the judgment to a guns kill. At any rate, his elation at scoring a kill was short-lived for his leader, Lt Cdr Cole Black, had been downed by the lead MiG-17.

Moments before Chancy's kill, having heard Black's call of "MiGs!", Smith and Vampatella (in his damaged Crusader) had hauled their jets around and sped back to the fight. As they closed, both noted two MiGs at 2,000ft in a diving right turn. Smith called a warning. "F-8, you have a MiG on your tail!" He could see the MiG's guns firing, followed by the F-8 bursting into flames. It was Cole Black going down. He and Lt Eastman were captured, and were not released until 1973.

A second MiG section then arrived. Smith went after the leader, but in a high-G turn his guns failed. Vampatella, meanwhile, had found another MiG saddled in on his tail, in gun range and firing. Vampatella tried to scissor with the MiG but the previous battle damage to his tail section limited his turns to 5Gs – the MiG stayed with him. Low fuel status or not, Vampatella lit his afterburner, disengaged from the MiG and headed east at 600 knots. Looking behind him, he saw that the enemy fighter had reversed course, apparently low on fuel itself. Vampatella reduced speed and turned back toward the departing MiG. From three-quarters-of-a-mile he fired one Sidewinder, then another (he only had two). The second missile detonated directly behind the MiG, ensuring its destruction. For his courage and skill, Lt(jg) Vampatella received the first Navy Cross given to a US Navy fighter pilot in Vietnam.

Upon the completion of this mission Capt Donaldson told Chancy to head for Saigon as the latest US Navy MiG killer. Later, a representative from Vought sent Chancy the MiG shooter lapel pin, which consisted of a plan view of an F-8 and a small red ruby signifying a MiG kill.

Ready for an Alpha strike in 1966, the aircraft and pilots of *Hancock*'s CVW-21 prepare to launch. NP 104, which Lt(jg) Phil Vampatella flew on his MiG-killing mission of June 21 that year, can just be seen with a raised canopy chained down between NP 102 and NP 108. The enlisted plane captain is hanging off the side of the cockpit ready to assist his pilot. (John Stewart)

A VF-211 lineup on the flightdeck of *Hancock* in 1966 shows, front row (from left to right), Tim Hubbard (MiG killer), Cole Black, Phil Vampatella (MiG killer), Bob Hulse, Gene Chancy (MiG killer), Phil Veeneman, Bill Rennie, Tom Brown and Bruce Henderson (maintenance). Back row, from left to right, Gene Jordan (maintenance), John Stewart (air intelligence), Tom Hall, Kay Russell, Spence Thomas, Hal Marr (MiG killer), "Miss Checkmate", Paul Speer (MiG killer), Richard Smith and Bill Nelson (senior maintenance officer). (US Navy)

It is worth noting that Lt Cdr Black's loss was definitely caused by a MiG-17, flown by Phan Van Tuc (although the VPAF also credit Phan Thanh Trung, Duong Truong Tan, and Nguyen Van Bay with his demise) also of the 923rd FR. It proved to be one of only four confirmed Crusader kills (three F-8s and one RF-8) credited to the MiG-17. The North Vietnamese list 12 F-8 claims, but these do not match US records. In addition to Lt Cdr Black, Cdr Dick Bellinger (CO of VF-162 aboard *Oriskany*) was shot down by a MiG-17 (flown by Ngo Duc Mai) on July 14, 1966. On September 5, 1966, former USAF F-102 and F-106 pilot, and now-exchange pilot, Capt Wilford K. Abbott, flying with VF-111 again from *Oriskany*, was lost to a MiG-17 flown by future seven-victory ace Nguyen Van Bay. Abbott was captured after ejecting and endured more than six years as a PoW. He and his wingman Lt Randy Rime had been bounced by two MiG-17s that came out of cloud cover and shot up both F-8s.

Although Rime was able to make it back to the carrier, Abbott's F-8 was more badly damaged. His cockpit was particularly badly shot up and he was also slightly wounded. When Abbot discovered that the controls of his fighter were quite sloppy he punched out.

I have consulted several published lists of losses and claims, and while the question exists as to the precise number of Crusaders lost to MiGs, the best answer remains only those four in the entire war. The VPAF still claims more, and recently several additional 'victories' have indeed been confirmed. It is doubtful any definitive word on either sides' claims will appear or be accepted by the opposing side.

The engagement in which Cdr Bellinger was shot down witnessed another dramatic confrontation between the Crusader and the MiG-17. Lt Cdr Chuck Tinker had launched as part of the planned four-plane division, Bellinger hoping to draw VPAF fighters out to go after the strikers, thus leaving themselves open to interception by the dedicated MiG-hunting F-8s. However, both of *Oriskany's* catapults had failed, leaving Tinker's wingman sitting on the deck. Weather conditions were not good either, forcing the three remaining F-8s to fly in between the cloud decks that were above and below them.

Just as *Red Crown* (the code name for the Positive Identification Radar Advisory Zone controller who provided US aircraft with radar coverage of North Vietnam via ship-mounted air search radar) called MiGs, Lt Dick Wyman spotted high-tailed fighters at "three o'clock". Tinker had just enough time to see a MiG closing from his "four o'clock" (his starboard rear quarter). The F-8 pilot broke hard right in a 6-8G turn to meet the threat, passing close enough so that he could see the enemy pilot. Unfortunately, his radio apparently failed right at that moment – the last call he heard was, "MiGs at 'three o'clock!'" Tinker could no longer communicate with

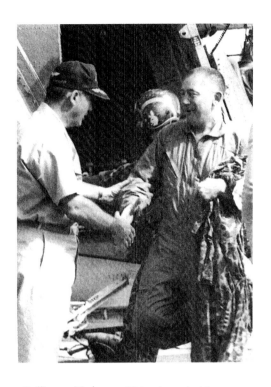

*Oriskany's* captain, John Iarrobino, welcomes VF-162's Cdr Dick Bellinger back after he had ejected from his F-8E on July 14, 1966. Bellinger's jet had been shot up by MiG-17F pilot Ngo Duc Mai of the 923rd FR. (US Navy)

his flight. Rolling hard left, he saw another MiG closing rapidly on Bellinger. Tinker intended to "cross the circle", hoping to set himself up for a Sidewinder shot. He had lost sight of Lt Wyman.

By now the MiG was shooting at Bellinger, and Tinker was desperate to rescue his CO. But a quick glance in his rearview mirrors alerted him to his own predicament – another MiG was right behind him at his "six o'clock". "The intake looked about the size of an open barn door", Tinker subsequently recalled. He broke hard left and

dove, making the MiG overshoot him. Tinker kept turning and descending out of the fight, going through the thin layer of clouds below him. When he cleared the deck he was only 600-800ft above the ground, and the MiG was still saddled in on his tail! Lt Cdr Tinker punched in his afterburner, hoping to escape the persistent MiG pilot. The F-8 still had plenty of fuel, so he knew he could stay in 'burner for a while as he skimmed over downtown Hanoi, all the while keeping his pursuer in his rearview mirrors. Then, suddenly, the VPAF pilot broke off and disappeared. Tinker never saw him again. Perhaps he was either low on fuel himself, or had had enough of the tail chase so low to the ground.

Nguyen Van Bay was one of the best-known VPAF aces, and included in his tally of seven kills was the RF-8A of VFP-63's Lt L. C. Eastman and the F-8E of VF-211's Lt Cdr Cole Black, both jets being downed on June 21, 1966. Bay shared these kills with three other pilots from the 923rd FR. He also claimed another F-8 on April 25, 1967, again with three other pilots, but on this occasion there was no corresponding loss according to US Navy records. Seen here wearing a leather SL-60 flying helmet, Bay has seven "Uncle Ho" badges, one for each kill, on his flying jacket. He served with the 923rd FR from 1966 through to 1972. (via Dr István Toperczer)

57

Joining up with the other two Crusaders from VF-162, he found that Cdr Bellinger's fighter was badly damaged and he was very low on fuel. Unable to refuel from a tanker, he was forced to eject and was eventually rescued.

## "BONNIE DICK'S" "FRESCO" KILLERS

The USS *Bon Homme Richard* (CVA-31), bearer of a proud old US Navy name, was a "27-Charlie" – a World War II-era *Essex* class fast carrier, now substantially modified and still a vital part of the US Navy's order of battle. CVW-21 aboard CVA-31 typified the "Charlies'" importance. On May 1, 1967, during a strike against Kep airfield, 35 miles north of Hanoi, Lt Cdr M. O. "Mo" Wright of VF-211 shot down one of three MiG-17s engaged by the unit. His wingman, USAF exchange pilot and former F-86 and F-100 driver Capt Ron Lord, spotted the enemy fighters beneath them, heading northeast towards China. Wright rolled in behind the third MiG and shot a Sidewinder up its tailpipe, sending the jet tumbling into the ground in four pieces – cockpit, two main wings and tail.

Lord, himself, chased a MiG off the tail of an A-4, telling the Skyhawk pilot to "Keep it moving. 'Nickle Four' has him" ("Nickle" was VF-211's tactical call sign). Lord rolled in behind the MiG as he listened to his Sidewinder's IR signals, but he could not tell if the missile was homing in on the A-4 or the MiG. He fired a short cannon burst in front of the enemy fighter and the tracers made the VPAF pilot break to the left. At 300-500ft above the ground, pulling 5Gs in a hard left turn, Capt Lord saw hits on the MiG's left wing and aft fuselage. It started trailing smoke and small pieces flew off it. Lord tried to keep the jet in sight, but he had to break up and away to avoid hitting a large jungle-covered hill.

His target was in afterburner and heading west towards the Northeast Railway – a major supply line from China protected by myriad flak sites. Lord could not follow the MiG and turned back towards his ship with Lt Cdr Wright. His MiG was classified

Five F-8 MiG killers pose in this photograph following CVW-21's highly successful 1967 cruise aboard CVA-31. These pilots are, from left to right, visiting USAF F-4C pilot Maj James A. Hargrove, who had downed a MiG-17 on May 14, 1967 using an SUU-16 20mm gun pod after firing Sidewinders and Sparrows at three other MiGs threatening a pair of F-105s, A-4C pilot Lt Cdr Ted Swartz of VA-76, who had shot down a MiG-17 with Zunis, and F-8 shooters Cdr Paul Speer, Lt Cdr M. O. Wright, Lt(jg) Joe Shea, Lt Cdr Bobby Lee and Lt Phil Wood. (US Navy)

as "damaged". Lord later completed an F-100 tour in South Vietnam followed by a stint flying USAF F-4s from Thailand. Following an Air War College assignment and three non-flying billets, he retired as a colonel in 1986.

The F-8's best days came next, when seven Crusaders shot down seven MiG-17s (nearly half the entire F-8 tally during the war). The two "Bonnie Dick" fighter squadrons each scored two MiG-17 kills on May 19, 1967. VF-24's Lt Cdrs Bobby Lee and Phillip Wood, in F-8Cs, and VF-211's CO, Cdr Paul Speer, and Lt(jg) Joseph Shea accomplished theirs with Sidewinders. The victories credited to Lee and Wood were the first for VF-24, although Wood was almost forced to eject from his Crusader shortly after claiming his kill. His jet, severely damaged and low on fuel, could not

VF-211's Ron Lord and "Mo" Wright point out the position of their fight where Lt Cdr Wright scored a kill and Lord a damaged credit. Their sweat-stained flight suits attest to the rigors of the engagement. (US Navy)

Phil Wood of VF-24 pre-flights one of his Crusader's AIM-9Ds on the flightdeck of "Bonnie Dick". He carried only three Sidewinders on his MiG engagement, the missile on the upper left rail having failed its preflight checks. The first weapon Wood fired was in the same position shown here, the lower left rail. (US Navy)

make it back to CVA-31, but he managed to land safely on *Kitty Hawk* – a ship he subsequently returned to in 1985 as its captain.

Two months later, on July 21, CVW-21 pilots scored again when A-4s set out on a strike against a POL (petroleum, oil and lubricants) storage facility at Ta Xa, northwest of Haiphong. When a VPAF flight of some ten MiG-17s attacked the bombers, the combined fighter escort from VF-24 and VF-211 knocked down three of the interceptors. One of the victorious pilots was VF-24's XO, Cdr Marion "Red" Isaacks, who almost became a victim himself when he stared for too long at the MiG's blazing fireball and allowed a second enemy fighter to close on him, firing all the way. Realizing his predicament just in the nick of time, Isaacks kicked right rudder and turned to meet his attacker. With his windscreen full of the MiG's gaping intake, Isaacks watched the VPAF pilot turn away at the last moment and snap-roll for the deck.

On his way back to the ship Isaacks did not know that he was being trailed by another MiG until VA-76's Lt Cdr T. R. Swartz, himself a recent MiG-17 killer after he had downed the VPAF fighter with Zuni rockets fired from his A-4, again tried a Zuni shot, this time between the F-8 and its pursuer. The startled MiG pilot abruptly pulled off and departed.

Phil Wood's F-8C (BuNo 147029) aboard *Kitty Hawk*. It was so badly damaged during his MiG encounter that it was struck from service, never to fly again. This photograph was taken by the pilot (Sam Sayers) of the A-6 that Lt Wood rescued from a MiG-17. Sayers autographed it, "A grateful A-6 pilot owes you a drink." (Phil Wood)

VF-24 XO Cdr "Red" Isaacks sits for a portrait in an F-8 hastily adorned with a temporary name sign shortly after he had claimed his MiG-17 on July 21, 1967. (US Navy)

Still on July 21, Jim Stockdale's LSO, Lt Cdr Tim Hubbard, had a rather strange mission loadout – only one AIM-9D and one pod of Zunis. His assigned aircraft had gone down before launch and he had to take another F-8 loaded for flak suppression duties, hence the rocket pod. But the Sidewinder had failed its post-launch check, leaving Hubbard with only the Zunis and his cannon. When eight MiGs attacked his section he turned hard left to meet the oncoming threat. Green tracers from behind told him he was under attack, and that the MiG pilot was using his big 37mm cannon. Hubbard turned hard again, forcing the enemy fighter to overshoot. Once behind the MiG he blasted away with his cannon before switching to his Zunis once he had exhausted his supply of ammunition. Coincidentally, Hubbard had been T. R. Swartz's escort on May 1, when the A-4 pilot got his MiG.

VPAF and North Korean fighter pilots run toward their MiGs at Kep. North Korean volunteers were the only other nationality to actually fly combat missions during the war for the VPAF. Several were lost, with at least three F-8 pilots scoring kills against MiG-17's flown by North Koreans – Lt Cdr "Mo" Wright on May 1, 1967 and Cdr "Red" Isaacks and Lt Cdr Tim Hubbard on July 21 that same year. It is also possible that a fourth was downed by Lt Cdr Robert Kirkwood on the latter date too, although information for Kirkwood's kill is inconclusive. In all three confirmed victories involving MiG-17's flown by North Koreans, the pilots were killed. (via Dr István Toperczer)

Lt Cdr Tim Hubbard on the side of a VF-211 F-8E. A highly capable, aggressive aviator, Hubbard was also a very colorful character. (US Navy)

Hubbard's first salvo missed, and he fired the two remaining rockets, one of which blew up close enough to cause major damage. As he pulled alongside the faltering MiG, he was surprised to see the VPAF pilot "flip him the bird" and eject just as his jet came apart. It was an incredible display of technique and fortitude, and perhaps more than any other engagement between the F-8 and MiG-17 showed the good and bad points of the individual aircraft and their respective pilots. It was also payback for Hubbard, who had been hit by flak on May 21 – struggling to make it back to his ship, he had had to eject when his F-8 caught fire. It is interesting to note that the pilots of the MiG-17s shot down by Wright, Isaacks, Lt Cdr Robert Kirkwood (of VF-24) and Hubbard were North Koreans, all probably with the rank of captain.

Tim Hubbard was one of the most colorful of all Crusader pilots. Well-liked by both the enlisted members of his squadron and other aviators, he had an equally colorful record that occasionally hindered him, especially at promotion time. In the 1970s his former CO, now Rear Adm Stockdale, recently returned from captivity in Hanoi, had to successfully step in to support his friend and former squadronmate to convince the board to promote Hubbard to commander.

Former F-8 pilot Cole Pierce summed it up:

> If the night was dark, the radio scratchy, the ceiling low, and the deck moving, the one voice you wanted to hear on the other end of the radio was Tim Hubbard.

## SCHAFFERT'S FIGHT

Perhaps the most extraordinary F-8/MiG-17 aerial engagement occurred during an A-4 *Iron Hand* escort mission on December 14, 1967. Two Crusader squadrons encountered what appeared to be a flight of the most aggressive and skillful MiG-17 pilots yet seen in the war. The lone VF-111 F-8C was flown by Lt Cdr Dick Schaffert, his jet being armed with three AIM-9Ds. The fourth missile had not checked out before launch, and he had had it removed to save weight. He told the author:

It was my first time carrying AIM-9Ds. The darn things weighed more than 200lb, which was the fuel required for a go-round during recovery, and I wanted to save the weight. After the fight I would have traded those three Ds for one old AIM-9B.

The "Sundowners" had flown F-8Es on their last Vietnam cruise (aboard *Oriskany* in 1966), but operational and combat losses along with limited numbers of "Echos" made it a toss-up as to whether VF-111 would retain them or not for the unit's next combat deployment. Thus, the toss of the dice at the Miramar O Club bar between the two COs of VF-162 and VF-111, who would deploy together in the *Oriskany*, decided the matter. Cdr "Cal" Swanson's three aces outbid Cdr Bob Rasmussen's pair, which meant the "Hunters" would get the new F-8Es while the "Sundowners" reverted to their earlier "Charlies". Dick Schaffert had not been too upset about the outcome, for it meant not having to tote heavy bombs. He and his squadronmates were fighter pilots again.

He recalls there was also a problem with the supply of AIM-9Ds that meant *Oriskany* still carried AIM-9Bs into January 1968. In the summer of 1967 there were very few "Delta" missiles on *Yankee Station*. If a particular ship's fighters were going where they were likely to encounter MiGs, helicopters transported the available AIM-9Ds to that vessel. "Based upon the fuzing failures of the 9D experienced during my and Rasmussen's firings on December 14, 1967", Schaffert told the author, "we preferred to carry the old but reliable 9B through to our departure from *Yankee Station* on January 28, 1968".

Schaffert was flying a loose-deuce position (to avoid AAA and "Fan Song" radar lock-on) on an A-4 flown by Lt(jg) Chuck Nelson on December 14. As they approached Thai Binh the "Fan Song" warning increased. Schaffert saw the pilot begin a pitch-up on a westerly heading – an indication that he was preparing to launch his Shrike anti-SAM missile. For this, the A-4 would be at 30 degrees, nose up and moving at 250 knots. To preclude slowing to Nelson's speed, Schaffert began a barrel roll – a displacement roll – around the A-4 at 350 knots. He was inverted at the top of the roll when he saw two MiG-17s two miles west of his position, slightly higher but diving. He called a "Tally-ho" to Nelson and took the lead.

Lt Cdr Schaffert was pursuing the lead section of MiGs in a high-G left turn when a second section slid in behind him. Tracers from the leader of the trailing jets streaked over his canopy. In that dire a situation, instinct should have told Schaffert to pull hard, putting on more Gs to throw the MiG leader out of position:

> However, I remembered an incident a few months before when MiG-17s had surprised two other VF-111 pilots [Lt Randy Rime and Capt Wil Abbott] by popping out of the clouds behind the F-8s. The Crusader pilots tried to out-turn the MiGs, which shot down one F-8.

Schaffert knew he could not escape by applying more Gs, so he shoved the stick forward, abruptly going from +6G to -2G – an incredible change in gravitational pull on the human body – while applying hard, left rudder to roll the nose of his F-8 under:

VF-111's Lt Cdr Dick Schaffert strikes a pose beside a "Sundowner" F-8C aboard *Oriskany* in 1967-68. Every way the depiction of a modern fighter pilot, he fought one of the most legendary engagements of the Vietnam War and lived to tell about it. Besides the normal fit of G-suit, torso harness and flight helmet, Schaffert also wears a camera around his neck – probably on loan from the squadron intelligence officer, although pilots often took their own cameras up so as to photograph subjects of interest. (via Dick Schaffert)

The MiGs didn't follow this erratic maneuver, and I did a vertical reversal to meet them head-on. We later found with captured MiG-17s that they couldn't perform a negative-G roll without going "squirrely". It was the first time I had tried it in the F-8.

VF-111 CO Cdr Bob Rasmussen was also there, escorting a VA-164 A-4 flown by Lt Cdr Denny Weichman. "We had been fishing in the area north of Haiphong for a SAM site", Rasmussen told the author, "when Bandit calls started coming out from *Red Crown*. A short time later Dick came up on my channel, and it was apparent he was the target of the bandits . . . or vice versa".

Rasmussen then took the lead from Weichman, suggesting that the A-4 pilot should head for the water while he raced back to help Schaffert. Although the latter was some 15 miles to the south, Rasmussen could clearly see the action. "Not because my eyes were that good", he explained, "but because of a phenomenon that I have yet to understand, and have never seen before or since. There was a distinct haze layer at about my altitude at 15,000ft. Clear as a bell above that level, and the usual North Vietnamese winter haze below". What he saw was a MiG-17 followed by an F-8, followed by another MiG-17. "What made it so easy to see was a distinct white trail behind each aircraft looking exactly like a heavy contrail all the way over the top of the maneuver and back into the haze, where the fight disappeared and stayed".

A few minutes later Rasmussen arrived on the scene. At this point it seemed that the MiGs had had enough of the wild man in the American Crusader (Schaffert), and were trying to disengage and head back up the Red River toward Hanoi. One MiG was flying low, perhaps 200ft above the ground, and making S-turns, snaking left to right. The second MiG had vanished. "The MiG pilot was really turning that bird, much tighter than I could", Rasmussen recalled. "I finally got a tone and launched the first 'winder. It did not track, probably because I was out of the tracking cone".

Rasmussen fired a second Sidewinder, which also failed, but the MiG pilot did not escape. Two VF-162 Crusaders flown by Cdr "Cal" Swanson and Lt Dick Wyman had joined the battle. As Rasmussen related, "Dick Wyman's 'winder caught him and he went into the rice paddy. I'd say that MiG pilot was a very competent driver flying a very capable aircraft". Cdr Swanson added, "That MiG pilot was a tiger. He was there to fight!"

It was now obvious that no one doubted the growing competency of VPAF pilots, who had gained considerably more combat experience, and commensurate skill – as the air war intensified. Nevertheless, AAA and SAMs still posed the greatest threat over

North Vietnam – of the 24 aircraft and 18 pilots lost in combat by CVW-21 during CVA-31's 112 days on the line in 1967, only one had fallen to a MiG.

Lt Cdr Schaffert received the DFC for his stalwart defense of the A-4s, and later went on to VF-92 to fly F-4Js. He arrived at his new squadron in time to fly several missions before VF-92 and its ship, *Constellation*, returned to the US in June 1972. Schaffert took command of the "Silver Kings" that August. Retiring as a captain, he earned his Ph.D., and remains active as an author and as an F-8 alumnus.

Rasmussen retired as a captain, and is presently the Director of the National Museum of Naval Aviation in Pensacola, Florida. His son is now also a captain and flies F/A-18 Hornets.

The F-8's next MiG-17 kill was not until July 9, 1968, when VF-191's Lt Cdr John Nichols escorted Lt William Kocar of VFP-63 (the US Navy's primary light photographic squadron) toward targets along the Song Ca River, having launched from *Ticonderoga*. As Kocar began his run at 2,000ft, Nichols, who was 1,000ft above him, spotted a camouflaged MiG-17 coming in almost dead behind the RF-8. Nichols radioed a warning and followed the enemy fighter into a hard turn. Immediately, tracers started streaking past him – he had not seen the MiG's wingman. Focusing on the lead fighter, Nichols fired a Sidewinder but the missile did not glide properly for he was too high above his target. The MiG pilot, however, unexpectedly stopped his turn, rolled wings level and lit his afterburner. Lt Cdr Nichols saddled in on the fighter's "six o'clock" (tail) and fired a second Sidewinder. This one hit, although the MiG surprisingly remained in the air. Nichols finished him off with his cannons.

Lt Dick Wyman was VF-162's Assistant Operations officer when he shot down a MiG-17 on December 14, 1967 following the incredible fight involving MiG-17s and pilots from two squadrons of F-8s, as well as a number of A-4s. (US Navy)

923rd FS pilots Luu Huy Chao, Le Hai, Mai Duc Toai and Hoang Van Ky were credited with downing an F-4B on April 24, 1967 (which US Navy records list as having fallen to AAA) and an F-105D the following day (again listed as having been downed by AAA). Both Chao and Hai finished the conflict with six aerial victories apiece in the MiG-17. According to VPAF records, Hai's final success, on July 19, 1968, was against an F-8, although none was listed as lost on this date by the US Navy. All four pilots are seen here wearing dark blue coats with a dark brown fur collar, as well as the winter version of the SL-60 black leather flying helmet and associated goggles. MiG-17F 2039 behind the pilots was regularly flown by ace Luu Huy Chao. (via Dr István Toperczer)

A green MiG-17 cuts across the North Vietnamese landscape during the epic encounter of December 14, 1967. One of a flight of four jets, the VPAF fighter was finally shot down by Lt Wyman of VF-162. (Chuck Nelson)

July 29, 1968 saw the final official (although not the last) Crusader/MiG-17 engagement, when a flight of four *Bon Homme Richard* F-8Es encountered four "Fresco-Fs". VF-53's section leader, Lt Cdr Guy Cane, and his wingman, Lt(jg) Dexter Manlove, met a two-MiG section head on and turned with the enemy fighters. Cane got off a Sidewinder, which detonated just behind the MiG's tailpipe. Cane later reported, "I thought it had missed until a chunk of his starboard wing came off and the MiG went into a nose-down spiral". It was Cane's 186th combat mission, but his first MiG encounter, and kill.

Two Crusader MiG-21 kills followed, one in August and one in September. By then the Phantom II had begun replacing the F-8 (which would soldier on until the ceasefire in 1973), and kills were scarce until 1972, when all the aerial victories fell to F-4 crews. The pilots still flying F-8s were all the more anxious for a crack at a MiG, and on May 23, 1972 Lt Jerry Tucker got his chance. With Lt Cdr Frank Bachman in the lead, the two were flying TARCAP (Target Combat Air Patrol) for an Alpha strike near the "Hourglass", south of Nam Dinh. The Alpha strike aircraft had completed their mission and were safely "feet wet", which left Bachman and Tucker time to look for enemy fighters prior to returning to *Hancock*.

Lt Cdr Guy Cane of VF-53 gestures appropriately from F-8E BuNo 150349 after returning to "Bonnie Dick" following his MiG-killing mission on July 29, 1968. The F-8's side number, 203, is barely discernable. (via Guy Cane)

Both pilots heard *Red Crown* (the GCI controller aboard the cruiser USS *Chicago* (CG-11)) vector two VF-161 Phantom IIs onto a MiG bogey heading south from "Bullseye" (Hanoi). They then heard the F-4 pilots report having lost sight of each other, and arranging a rendezvous circle to rejoin, before continuing toward the MiG. It was at this point that Lt Tucker told *Red Crown* that his section was ready to go, resulting in the GCI controller calling off the Phantom IIs and sending in the Crusaders instead.

Tucker and Bachman spotted the MiG-17 north of them and maneuvered for the intercept. Tucker, with the enemy fighter in sight, had the lead. The MiG was low, heading south and moving fast. As he began his turn behind the VPAF fighter, Tucker's AIM-9D Sidewinder

Lt Jerry Tucker of VF-211 prepares for a mission on *Hancock's* flightdeck in 1972. The plane captain (right) has pulled the safety pins from the F-8's ejection seat, which is now armed. (John Stewart)

began to growl, the missile's seeker head "sniffing" its quarry. An instant later, for whatever reason, the MiG's canopy flew off, immediately followed by the airplane's occupant, Nguyen Cong Ngu of the 923rd FR – scratch one MiG. Although Hanoi does acknowledge the probability of a MiG-17 and F-8 confrontation on the day in question, the US Navy denied Tucker credit for the kill. Neither pilot had fired at the MiG. Oddly enough, however, *Hancock* did get credit for its overall kill total.

There were other similar "engagements", but denied as it was, Jerry Tucker's and Frank Bachman's encounter with the MiG-17 was the last Crusader-claimed kill.

Lt(jg) Henry Livingston, another member of VF-211, had come close to downing a MiG-17 on March 7, 1972. He and Lt Cdr Ed Schrump had launched on a BARCAP (Barrier Combat Air Patrol), with the latter pilot as the designated flight leader. They each had 200 rounds of 20mm cannon ammunition and two AIM-9Ds. Later in the war the F-8s flew with 25 rounds per gun less than in the early deployments, and the earlier loadout of four Sidewinders was often reduced to two, mainly because the additional pair of missiles created an unacceptable drag. Indeed, in Lt(jg) Livingston's opinion – and probably others – the extra weapons "made the airplane such a dog". He explained to the author:

Lt Tucker's MiG "Scarer", F-8J BuNo 150900, on a CAP mission in 1972 armed with two Sidewinders and bearing the 101 modex of Cdr Jim Davis, VF-211's CO, on its nose. (US Navy)

One of the great advantages of the F-8 was its ability to escape a losing situation. As you lost turn to an attacker you could elect to start nose down in a turn into him, droops up, light the 'burner and then unload as much as you could so as not to lose sight of the attacker behind you. As long as you could see him, you were extending nose to tail on most enemy aircraft because the F-8 could accelerate so much faster than most. At about three to five miles you put the droops down, came out of 'burner and pitched back over the top to re-commence the attack head-on, or better. With four 'winders, the drag was enough to really screw up this maneuver and prevent hard-G turns into a fight without losing a lot of energy.

Schrump and Livingston rendezvoused and climbed to 20,000ft. They checked in with *Red Crown* aboard *Chicago*, which was responsible for northern Tonkin Gulf forward air control throughout most of the war. *Red Crown* immediately called out a MiG advisory just as they saw two contrails coming from the opposite direction. It was the returning BARCAP from VF-24, their sister squadron aboard *Hancock*. The "Red Bandit" call ("Red Bandit" indicated a MiG-17, while "Blue Bandit" was for a MiG-21) was followed with a heading and distance from "Bullseye", the code name for Hanoi.

Schrump and Livingston decided to keep their power setting at military rating thrust (MRT), which offered less fuel consumption than combat rating thrust (CRT) or afterburner. Also, MRT did not create the characteristic large white puff of 'burner ignition, which could have alerted the MiG pilot. Lt Cdr Schrump passed the lead to his wingman because Livingston had a better, or "sweet", radar.

The initial MiG call was only 20 miles dead-on ahead of the two F-8s. With closure speeds in excess of 1,100mph, or about 18 miles a minute, the two Crusader pilots were scanning the cloud-layered horizon intensely. Lt(jg) Livingston abruptly asked Lt Cdr Schrump to switch communications with *Chicago* to "secure voice". He wanted to ask for more information without that transmission being heard by anyone else. Livingston needed to be sure that there was only one MiG in the area. Something did not smell right. He asked the controller aboard the cruiser if he saw any other contacts, any more MiGs in the area. The controller immediately came back with an affirmative – there were six "Blue Bandits" in trail behind the "Red Bandit"! In other words, six MiG-21s were set up as a trap by flying high and behind the MiG-17, which was the bait. Nevertheless, Livingston and Schrump pressed on.

In seconds, the enemy was within ten miles. At that point, oddly, the MiG-17's southward progress became a 180-degree turn across the Crusaders' noses and back toward the north. Lt(jg) Livingston quickly shut down his radar to keep from warning the enemy. As *Red Crown* called the MiGs closing to five miles, the controller warned the two Crusader pilots that they would have to soon break it off and turn around because they were approaching "a no-go latitude" – a boundary beyond which was a forbidden area, one of the leftovers from meddling in Washington, D.C. preventing American aircraft from pursuing their quarry. Seven years earlier, Bud Flagg of VF-162 had run into the same problem. The VF-211 pilots faced deteriorating visual conditions and then, at three miles, they were called off by *Red Crown*. Livingston said later that he thought he would have other chances, but this episode would be as close to a kill as he would ever get.

# STATISTICS AND ANALYSIS

While the F-8 was active throughout the entire Vietnam War, it mainly fought VPAF MiG-17s between 1965 and 1968. During the final years of the conflict the Crusader had largely been supplanted by the F-4 Phantom II, the Vought fighter only serving on the smaller "27C" carriers (principally *Hancock* and *Oriskany*) that could not handle the much larger and heavier F-4. Any modifications necessary to make these vessels suitable for the Phantom II were deemed to be too costly for older carriers on their final deployments prior to retirement.

During Operation *Rolling Thunder*, which President Lyndon B. Johnson halted on October 31, 1968, US Navy F-8s had officially shot down 18 VPAF MiGs, of which 14 were MiG-17s, for the official loss of three F-8s and one RF-8. Thus, the exchange rate was approximately six-to-one. If the total includes Hal Marr's second MiG and Jerry Tucker's "scare" kill, bringing the total to 20 kills for the F-8, the ratio is nearly seven-to-one. No such one-sided numbers have ever been achieved by any other American fighter. Of course, VPAF MiG-17 pilots claimed quite a few more F-8s downed – 11 to be precise – but seven of these losses cannot be substantiated by US records.

US Navy squadrons lost only a few F-4s while bringing down 15 MiGs, including nine MiG-17s. Seven more kills were unconfirmed or "probables". Of course, US Navy (and one US Marine Corps) F-4 crews shot down a lot more MiGs over a longer period. Numbers rise and fall depending on what sources are used, but there is no denying that victories were achieved. US Navy flight tactics stuck with the tried-and-true "loose deuce" formation, which provided for the simple flight leader protected by

Lt(jg) Tom Hall prepares for a mission in NP 101, which was Cdr Paul Speer's F-8E – note the MiG kill flag beneath the cockpit. Hall was shot down by AAA and captured on June 10, 1967. He had also been downed four days earlier, on June 6, but on that occasion he had been rescued. Hall was released in March 1973. Lt(jg) John Stewart, the squadron air intelligence officer and an F-8 pilot himself, hangs off the side to pose with his close friend. Hall's helmet carries a well-known jibe at the time, FUBIJAR (Fuck You Buddy! I'm Just a Reserve!), which was meant as a taunt from the Naval Reserve commissioned aviators who populated a large portion of the junior officer ranks at the height of the war (John Stewart)

his wingman. The VPAF sent four-plane formations into an engagement, loosely crediting each pilot with the kill if the American jet was brought down.

With the end of *Rolling Thunder*, each side was afforded a much-needed breathing space in which to assess their tactics, refresh and re-supply their lineups and retrain their crews. While spending a two-week jet introduction course at NAS Kingsville in late October/early November 1968, the author remembers the cessation of the *Rolling Thunder* campaign. It had been a long, hard-fought three-and-a-half years. Many men and aircraft had been lost, and the bombing halt did not sit well with the instructors, many of whom had just returned from Vietnam where they had lost friends and compatriots. The morning after the announcement, the lieutenants' smiles and jokes of the previous days were gone, and the gloom lasted for the rest of the course.

| MiG-17 Kills by Type | | |
|---|---|---|
| F-8 Crusader | F-4 Phantom II | F-105D/F Thunderchief |
| June 1966-September 1968 | June 1965-January 1973 | June 1966-December 1967 |
| 18 (excluding two unofficial or later official kills, one for VF-211 on June 12, 1966 by Cdr Hal Marr; and one for VF-211 on May 23, 1972 by Lt Jerry Tucker – it would appear that in a semi-official list issued by the VPAF even the North Vietnamese admit to the loss of Marr's second MiG. | 19 (US Navy and US Marine Corps)<br><br>33 (USAF) | 27 |

Although Lt Cdr "Mo" Wright did not claim his MiG-17 (on May 1, 1967) in this jet, it was assigned to him later in "Bonnie Dick's" 1967 war cruise and duly given a MiG-kill decal below the cockpit. At this time Wright was the Safety Officer for VF-211, and the fourth most senior officer in the squadron. (Cole Pierce)

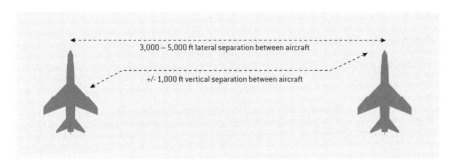

3,000 – 5,000 ft lateral separation between aircraft

+/- 1,000 ft vertical separation between aircraft

| MiG-21 Kills by Type | |
|---|---|
| **F-8 Crusader** | **F-4 Phantom II** |
| 4 | 12 (US Navy and US Marine Corps) |
| | 66 (USAF) |

| Other VPAF Kills by Type | |
|---|---|
| **MiG-19** | **An-2** |
| 2 (US Navy F-4) | 2 (US Navy F-4) |
| 6 (USAF F-4) | |

The F-8 did not have much of a chance to participate in the post-*Rolling Thunder* engagements that followed the establishment of the Navy Fighter Weapons School, better known as Topgun, at NAS Miramar. Yet, for a time, US Navy Crusader squadrons were the "keepers of the flame" that still burned in the hearts of American fighter pilots. It had been so before the war, before the first combat deployments to Southeast Asia, and it remained this way well into the conflict until the mission of fighter combat was taken away from the remaining F-8 pilots and given to other communities.

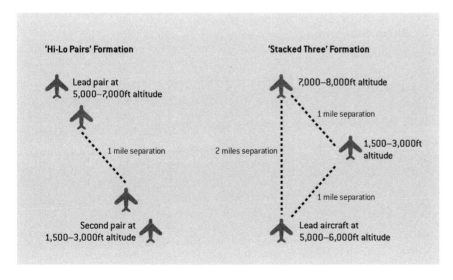

'Hi-Lo Pairs' Formation

Lead pair at 5,000–7,000ft altitude

1 mile separation

Second pair at 1,500–3,000ft altitude

'Stacked Three' Formation

7,000–8,000ft altitude

1 mile separation

1,500–3,000ft altitude

2 miles separation

1 mile separation

Lead aircraft at 5,000–6,000ft altitude

"Loose deuce" was the primary tactical doctrine used by US Navy fighters in the Vietnam War. It was similar in concept to the Thach Weave of World War II, but adapted to an offensive rather than defensive tactic, changing the traditional wingman's role of protecting the leader's rear to offensive maneuvering, thus increasing pressure on the adversary and bringing gun/missile power to bear during an engagement. The two F-8s flew with the wingman abeam of the leader, with 3,000-5,000ft separation, and 1,000ft above or below the lead. The Section Leader, designated Military Lead, remained in command of the flight, but could surrender control during an engagement to his free-maneuvering wingman, who, in a cover position, watched to see if the leader began to lose the tactical advantage, or called the free-fighter to engage. At that point, the wingman became Tactical Lead until such time as he either killed the bandit or began to lose tactical advantage. The engagement then became a series of vertical maneuvers to convert potential energy or recover potential energy by the pair, all the while maintaining constant pressure on the adversary.

MiG-17s usually flew four-aircraft formations in two pairs, and each pair would often fly closer together, appearing on radar as a single "blip". The low altitude pair would hope to approach US strike formations unnoticed against the background terrain, and they would climb into the action once the leading pair had mounted their attack. A three-aircraft formation in which a "trailer" jet would attack while the lead pair distracted the enemy was an adaptation of the tactic used by MiG-21 units. Often, the two types worked together using this method.

Groundcrew prepare an F-8 for a mission over North Vietnam in April 1968. The cramped space on a 27C carrier is fairly evident from this photograph. The sailor near the F-8's missiles – four are mounted – carries tie-down chains used to keep aircraft securely in place on a pitching flightdeck. (US Navy)

Yet the US Navy and the USAF knew who still had the fire. Col Robin Olds, the leading light in the USAF's MiG killer ranks, had been highly dissatisfied with his group's performance, and when he had returned from a mission, throwing his flight helmet out of the cockpit before climbing from his F-4, he knew where to go for help. Olds had four MiGs to his credit to add to his tally of 13 kills in World War II as a P-38 and P-51 pilot. Some people believe his total in Vietnam was actually higher, and that he was probably the war's first American ace, but he did not press the fact because he knew that such a designation would immediately take him out of combat. So in August 1972 a group of VF-24 pilots, led by MiG killer John Nichols, went to the Royal Thai Air Base at Udorn to conduct an airborne seminar for the USAF's F-4 squadrons so as to show their blue-suit brethren how it was done.

However, by this time, the Crusader's career was finished. While the F-4 produced two pilot aces (one each in the US Navy and USAF) and three back-seater aces (one in the US Navy and two in the USAF), the highest number of kills officially credited to F-8 drivers was one. There were several Crusader pilots who claimed mighty attractive probables, like Hal Marr and Tim Hubbard, but the published lists remain one kill for each of the official F-8 shooters. On the other hand, VPAF MiG-17 aces, of which the number varies, only claimed one, maybe two F-8s, and others admitted to only a few F-8 engagements.

| VPAF MiG-17 Aces with at least one F-8 score | |
|---|---|
| Nguyen Van Bay | 7 total, including one RF-8 shared and two F-8Es shared |
| Luu Huy Chao | 6 total, including one F-8 shared and 1 unconfirmed by US records |
| Le Hai | 6 total, including one F-8E unconfirmed by US records |

An interesting note concerns the individual firings of various ordnance (guns and missiles but not unguided rockets) by both sides courtesy of the *Red Baron* reports published by the Weapons System Evaluation Division of the Institute of Defense Analysis after the war to describe and dissect each aerial engagement of the conflict.

The MiG-17 fired its cannons some 340 times, and launched perhaps 76 aerial missiles. The MiG-21, by contrast, fired at least 344 missiles, while firing its cannon only 35 times. Obviously, the MiG-21 had a much higher success rate with missiles, while the MiG-17 proved more potent with its heavy cannon. In fact, the MiG-17 had only one missile kill, while the MiG-21 saw only one gun kill, but enjoyed a number of missile kills. MiG-17s began carrying missiles much later in the war, and many of the earlier engagements were with jets armed exclusively with their internal cannon. F-8 firing data is occasionally clouded by the lack of dependability of its four Colt 20mm cannon, as well as the similar unpredictability of the AIM-9 Sidewinder. When both weapons worked as advertised, they did very well, often in combination.

As previously noted in this volume, Le Hai scored six kills, although his F-8 claim over the 4th Military District on July 19, 1968 cannot be confirmed by US records. (via Dr István Toperczer)

VF-211's NP 112 wears the name *Bear* on its fuselage, which was the call sign of Lt Richard Amber who had been badly hurt in a ramp strike on March 16, 1971. A popular member of the squadron, he survived his mishap but was paralyzed and medically retired. Carrying AIM-9Ds, this F-8J is also flying a mission in March 1971 shortly before Amber's mishap. (US Navy)

# AFTERMATH

A direct comparison between the F-8 and the F-4 during the Vietnam War cannot be made without several qualifications that dilute the overall match-up. Certainly, each aircraft, and the men who flew them, were the best in their class. The F-8, however, was always a fighter, occasionally a fighter that could carry other ordnance than bullets, but first and always a fighter. And Crusader pilots, first and foremost, were always fighter pilots.

The F-4, on the other hand, had many more tasks assigned to it, and it became a fighter-bomber, successful in both roles. Then there was the time that each aircraft was serving in the war. While the Crusader saw action first, beginning with the Gulf of Tonkin Incidents in August 1964, the Phantom II equipped more squadrons and was in frontline action longer, and was, therefore, afforded more opportunities to fight MiGs. So, while the Crusader's official list of 18 kills (14 MiG-17s and 4 MiG-21s) may look a little meager beside the US Navy (and US Marine Corps) F-4's 35 (including two An-2s), there are many other factors to consider.

Phantom II crews did not train as much as Crusader pilots in air combat maneuvering (ACM). This was especially true of the USAF's F-4 crews, but also the US Navy's to a lesser extent. It was not until the US Navy set up Topgun, watched closely and enviously by the USAF, that the old feelings about fighter-to-fighter combat returned. By the busy months of 1972, when US Navy crews engaged MiGs more frequently and gained more kills, it was obvious that the ACM training was of great value. The USAF created its *Red Flag* exercises that addressed several communities and derived great benefit from the increased and revised training.

When the Vietnam War ended in a ceasefire in March 1973, and most American forces either withdrew completely from the area, or at least maintained patrols in the South China Sea – much as the situation had been in 1964 before the incidents with

North Vietnamese PT boats – the F-8 had only a few more years to serve. When finally retired from the Fleet, surviving jets saw out their days with the US Navy Reserve before again being replaced by the F-4. The older "27-Charlie" carriers *Hancock* and *Oriskany* made their last cruises in 1975, taking the F-8 – but not the RF-8 – with them into retirement. *Hancock* was nearby when, in May 1975, communist Khmer Rouge forces captured the US container ship SS *Mayaguez*, precipitating a bloody rescue mission to release the crewmen. The RF-8 soldiered on until 1982, when it and its squadron, VFP-63, were finally retired to make room for the new F-14 Tomcat and its TARPS capabilities.

For their part, the VPAF's MiG-17 fighter regiments continued fighting, even though their little jet fighters were showing their age compared to newer models of the MiG-21 that kept arriving. The MiG-17 was still a valuable close-in fighter and, much like the Japanese Zero-sen of World War II, when handled by an experienced pilot it could still offer a dangerous response to any US fighter. In fact, the last MiG claim of the conflict was made on January 12, 1973 by a VF-161 crew (pilot Lt Victor Kovaleski and RIO Lt(jg) Jim Wise), who shot down a MiG-17. The VPAF listed 17 aces (including four MiG-17 aces and 13 MiG-21 aces), the best of which was MiG-21 pilot Nguyen Van Coc with nine kills. He eventually rose to command the VPAF later in his career. North Vietnamese kills had to be confirmed with gun camera films along with witnesses, as well as wreckage. US Navy requirements included witnesses or intelligence sources. It was still somewhat nebulous.

All in all, F-8 pilots had done very well in the limited time they had had in-theater, and with the number of opportunities and "vectors" toward MiGs. Whereas most MiG-21 engagements were direct confrontations, those involving the smaller and slower MiG-17s often developed into more of an old-fashioned dogfight where, unfortunately for the VPAF pilots, their lack of experience showed.

As one writer has pointed out, the simplicity of the MiG-17 compared to the complex design and equipment of the F-8 and F-4 was often a great advantage, and it gave the MiG a robustness that brought the plane and its pilot home, even though it might have seemed to its attackers that the fighter was going down. This simplicity also facilitated an equally simple maintenance schedule that was unknown to the American maintainers aboard the crowded carriers in the South China Sea.

The MiG-17 continued to serve throughout the 1980s, usually in the ground-attack role. Fighter duties had been passed on to the MiG-21 by 1973, with increasing numbers of these supersonic fighters relegating the surviving "Fresco-C/Ds" to training duties.

Standing out on the 921st FR flightline at Noi Bai in 1972, this war-weary MiG-17 is painted in green with gray "splotches". A line-up of MiG-21 single- and two-seat trainers is in the background. Illustrating how the venerable "Fresco" was being re-roled as a ground attack platform and leaving the interception mission to the "Fishbed", 2072 is armed with ORO-57K unguided rocket pods rather than the usual PTB-400 drop tanks. (via Dr István Toperczer)

# FURTHER READING

**Books**

Barthelmes, Ed, *Walk Around F-8 Crusader* (Squadron/Signal No 38, 2005)

Davies, Peter, *Osprey Duel 23 – USN F-4 Phantom II vs VPAF MiG-17/19 Vietnam 1965-73* (Osprey, 2009)

Gilcrist, P., *Crusader! Last of the Gunfighters* (Schiffer, 1995)

Ginter, Steve, *Vought's F-8 Crusader – Navy Fighter Squadrons* (Naval Fighters No 19, 1990)

Green, William and Swanborough, Gordon, *The Observer's Soviet Aircraft Directory* (Frederick Warne Co., 1975)

Green, William and Pollinger, Gerald, *The World's Fighting Planes, Third and Revised Edition* (Hanover House, 1959)

Hobson, Chris, *Vietnam Air Losses (*Midland Publishing, 2001)

Mersky Peter, *Osprey Combat Aircraft 7 – F-8 Crusader Units of the Vietnam War* (Osprey, 1998)

Mersky, Peter, *Osprey Combat Aircraft 12 – RF-8 Crusader Units Over Cuba and Vietnam* (Osprey, 1998)

Monier, Chris, *F-8 Crusader BuNo 149210 and Its Drivers, The Amazing Tale of a US Fighter Jet Throughout the Vietnam War* (Escape, 2013)

Nguyen Sy Hung, et al. *Air Engagements in the Skies Over Vietnam (1965-1975)* (People's Army Publishing House, 2013)

Nichols, John and Tillman, Barrett, *On Yankee Station – The Naval Air War Over Vietnam* (Naval Institute Press, 1987)

Stapfer, Hans-Heiri, *MiG-17 Fresco in Action* (Squadron/Signal No 125, 1992)

Tillman, Barrett, *MiG Master – The Story of the F-8 Crusader* (Nautical & Aviation Publishing Company of America, 1980)

Tillman, Barrett, with Henk van der Lugt, *Osprey Aviation Elite Units 36 – VF-11/111 'Sundowners' 1942-95* (Osprey, 2010)

Toperczer, István, *Air War Over North Vietnam* (Squadron/Signal, 1998)

Toperczer, István, *Osprey Combat Aircraft 25 – MiG-17 and MiG-19 Units of the Vietnam War* (Osprey, 2001)

Toperczer, István, *Osprey Combat Aircraft 29 – MiG-21 Units of the Vietnam War* (Osprey, 2002)

**Documentary Sources**

NATOPS Flight Manual NAVAIR

**Periodicals**

Buza, Zoltan and Toperczer, István, *MiG-17 Over Vietnam* (Wings of Fame, Volume 8)

Buza, Zoltan and Toperczer, István, *MiG-19 in the Vietnam War* (Wings of Fame, Volume 11)

Department of the US Air Force, *Aces & Aerial Victories – The United States Air Force in Southeast Asia 1965-1973.* (USAF HQ, 1976)

Department of the Navy, *Naval Aviation News* (various issues)

Mersky, Peter, *Vought F-8 Crusader* (Wings of Fame, Volume 5)

The Tailhook Association, *The Hook* (various issues)

# INDEX

References to illustrations are shown in **bold**.